Series / Number 04-021

Cultural Diversity and the American Experience: Political Participation Among Blacks, Appalachians, and Indians

JOHN PAUL RYAN
American Judicature Society

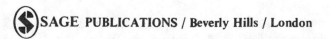

$)$SAGE PUBLICATIONS / Beverly Hills / London

For information address:

SAGE PUBLICATIONS, INC.
275 South Beverly Drive
Beverly Hills, California 90212

SAGE PUBLICATIONS LTD
St George's House / 44 Hatton Garden
London EC1N 8ER

International Standard Book Number 0-8039-0479-7

Library of Congress Catalog Card No. 74-19993

FIRST PRINTING

When citing a professional paper, please use the proper form. Remember to cite the
correct Sage Professional Paper series title and include the paper number. One of the
two following formats can be adapted (depending on the style manual used):

(1) NAGEL, S. S. (1973) "Comparing Elected and Appointed Judicial Systems."
Sage Professional Papers in American Politics, 1, 04-001. Beverly Hills, and London:
Sage Pubns.

OR

(2) Nagel, Stuart S. 1973. *Comparing Elected and Appointed Judicial Systems.* Sage
Professional Papers in American Politics, vol. 1, series no. 04-001. Beverly Hills and
London: Sage Publications.

CONTENTS

Cultural Diversity and the American Experience: Political Participation Among Blacks, Appalachians, and Indians

JOHN PAUL RYAN
American Judicature Society

INTRODUCTION

The American experience has most often been portrayed as a "melting pot"—people of diverse ethnic, racial, and cultural backgrounds coming to the United States to share in a common search for the religious, economic, and personal freedoms which they could not find elsewhere—in short, searching for the American Dream.[1] Certainly, the federal government has done its share to make this impossible dream come true. Conscious of the need for societal stability, the new American government set out to eliminate multiple languages, life-styles, and value-structures.[2] Blacks were transformed from persons into property; Indians were slaughtered or removed to (then) unwanted and isolated reservations; western and eastern European immigrants were "assimilated." But almost as quickly as the social fabric was being woven, it was also becoming unstrung. Blacks were declared "emancipated," Indians were deserving of federal services, women were worthy of political roles. The conquered were liberated. Or were they?

If the flow of events in the nineteenth century is historically understandable for the young nation-state, the spectacle of the twentieth

AUTHOR'S NOTE: *This is a revised version of a paper delivered at the 1973 American Political Science Association Meetings in New Orleans, Louisiana. For comments on various earlier drafts of this paper, I am grateful to numerous colleagues, but especially to Professor Herbert Jacob.*

century seems more puzzling. Indian children are physically beaten in the reservation schools as they dare to speak in their native tribal tongues; Hispanic children receive similar treatment in urban schools; Japanese-Americans (seemingly without regard for their life-situation or "patriotism") are "relocated" during World War II; Blacks are denied the most elementary right in a democratic society—the right to vote; and nearly all cultural minority groups are stereotyped and ridiculed over communications media which are licensed by the federal government.

How is it, then, that such events occur in a constitutionally stable democracy? Is it because the popular majority needs to be reinforced, indeed convinced, that its life-style is the most consonant with national symbols?[3] Or is it because the government still fears that the forces of cultural pluralism are a threat to nationalism and, ultimately, a threat to the ruling elite? Whatever the reasons for the persistence of the doctrine of consensus, activists and practitioners in politics argue (by their words and deeds) that the *failure* to acknowledge a validity to racial and ethnic identities or referents, when articulated or demanded, has its own set of consequences for societal integration and institutional effectiveness. In this latter vein, Cleaver (1968) and George Jackson (1970) make the argument with respect to American prisons, Deloria (1969) for parts of the federal bureaucracy, urban decentralizationists (Lindsay) for public schools, and community organizers (Alinsky, Jesse Jackson, Baraka) for public services generally. And in a recent commentary on the American experience, Dixon and Foster (1971) argue that a national identity synonymous only with "Euro-American" identity cannot represent adequately American society in the future. They set forth the alternative of a "union of different cultures—Black, Indian, Chinese, Chicano, Euro-American" to define the national identity, and implicitly suggest that an explanation and understanding of America present and past must be rooted in these differing cultural experiences. Despite the mumblings of successful politicians on election nights—"Tonight, I see the face of a child. . . he is black, he is white; he is Mexican, Italian, Polish. None of that matters . . . he is an American child," (Nixon, 1968)—perhaps there can be no American Dream, but only multiple and different dreams which have their roots in the concordance between cultural heritage and national loyalty.

SOCIAL SCIENCE:
WHICH VISION IS TO BE REPRESENTED?

In both normative and empirical voices, though rarely in unison, social science has intruded into this lofty debate about the American experience. Contemporary empirical research, particularly that focusing on "political behavior," has subtly and perhaps unwittingly chosen its side. The vision of America to be represented is one of marginal diversity within the framework of fundamental homogeneity and consensus—one political culture. Thus, the authors of *The People's Choice, Voting, The American Voter, Participation in America,* and ironically, *The Civic Culture* all conceptualized, sampled, and analyzed their data as if only one social system or experience were operative in the United States. In the early Columbia studies (Berelson, 1954; Lazarsfeld, 1944), the goal was to discover the dynamics of the voting decision itself among individuals (from a panel study) and to generalize this psychological process to all Americans. For Campbell (1964), the goal was to describe a "national electorate" through national probability sampling. The result, we are told, is not only an account of two presidential elections but a "funnel of causality" which can explain statistically most of the variation in presidential voting choices among Americans. Verba and Nie (1972), while expanding the range of political activities beyond voting and the immediate electoral arena, similarly utilized a national probability sample to analyze the correlates of participation, and in so doing analyze Black-White differences at the individual level within one common frame of reference. And for Almond and Verba (1963), though the task was a comparative study of five nations including the United States, the guiding assumption remained that cross-national diversity was more significant than within-nation diversity. What links these (and other) studies together is their self-fulfilling conviction, reflected in methodological assumptions, that most Americans are basically alike in their "common" heritage, democratic and electoral values, individualistic life-style, nuclear family, and so on. Yes, it is conceded that Blacks don't participate in certain kinds of electoral political activities as often as Whites, but they would if only they hadn't been discriminated against. Thus, Matthews and Prothro (1966) prefer to hang onto their Guttman scale of political participation (which doesn't scale very well for Blacks) rather than suggesting that "systems differ"—that acts which may be appropriate and gratifying in the political realm for Whites may not be (and may never be) for Southern Blacks. Yes, it is noted that Blacks display lower rates of political efficacy than Whites but both groups are assumed to have an equivalent attitudinal construct called "political efficacy" which can be measured by the same set of attitude items (language stimuli).[4] And so it goes—the prevailing research states that the distribution of particular styles of political behavior or socio-political attitudes may differ from group to group, but all groups within the national boundaries of the United States still belong to one attitudinal or behavioral *system* or set.

There have been a number of critiques of political behavior research, particularly the voting studies. Natchez (1970) suggests that the SRC studies were insufficiently guided by theory in the initial stages of conceptualization, a charge which receives empirical support from Shaffer's (1972) computer simulations using voting behavior data. Prewitt and Nie (1970) note that the low frequency of political participation which the SRC found among Americans may be partial methodological artifact. And Rossi (1959) charges that the methodological designs of the Columbia studies were partially inappropriate for testing the propositions advanced, and that the SRC-Michigan work suffered from incomplete data analysis after more appropriate linkages between theory and design. But few have charged that within-nation diversity in the United States is so great as to render the resultant empirical findings difficult to interpret, indeed quite easy to misinterpret.

In effect, Przeworski and Teune (1970) have laid the groundwork for the possibility of arriving at this conclusion. In *The Logic of Comparative Social Inquiry,* these authors argue that cross-cultural comparisons are more slippery than had once been realized. Equivalence cannot be established merely by sterile translations of questionnaires but must be achieved by concept comparability, an intricate process that demands empirical testing of indicators for cross-cultural application. Then, systems are to be compared not simply on the basis of frequency distributions (such as, which society reflects higher levels of voting, political participation, political efficacy) but pattern interrelationships (that is, do the same variables interrelate and cluster in similar or varying ways in different societies?) For example, is frequency of political participation a function of race in one society, but of educational achievement in a second society? If such is the case, do race and education represent "equivalent" indicators of social status in the two societies, or must the level of explanation be raised to the system (in this instance, nation) for an answer? In sum, Przeworski and Teune (1970) argue for new ways of measuring "similar" phenomena in different cultures as well as different criteria for establishing whether the cultures (systems) differ. Although the examples cited in their work are primarily cross-national, the application of the "logic" of comparative inquiry to a within-nation focus seems highly appropriate, potentially offering a different perspective on the consensus versus cleavage debate within the American political system.

Finally, there is some limited-focus empirical research which suggests the utility of a within-system framework for studying political behavior in the United States. For example, contrast two socialization studies of different geographic scope: drawing upon a nationally-based, urban, middle-class sample of youth, Hess and Torney (1967) found a benevolent, strongly positive image of the President among American children; a subcultural replication (Jaros, 1968) uncovered a stunning reversal of this image of the President among rural, Appalachian white children. And Easton and Dennis (1969) in a theoretical reconceptualization of the Hess-Torney data stress the significance of the depth of diffuse support for the political system among American youth; but Keniston (1960) in an early work finds a segment of American youth undecided about large parts of the American value structure, then discovers the evolution of at least part of the "doubters" into a group committed to quite different political and social values and personal strategies (Keniston, 1968). And in a study of the role of bio-chemical agents (drugs) in political socialization, Jaros (1972) provides limited evidence from an experimental setting to suggest that the "high" generation may be undergoing a process of "desocialization" or "depoliticization," possibly resulting in large vacuums of the diffuse support upon which the stability of the political system allegedly rests. Lastly, Jacob (1972) in a broad survey of ghetto Blacks, middle-class Whites, and working-class Whites finds that the consumption of government services—in both frequency and quality—differs from group to group, as do the effects of contact with government officials on individual political attitudes.

More empirical research, utilizing still different approaches, suggests the viability of within-system foci. Liebow (1967), in participant observation of black, male, streetcorner society in an urban ghetto, found that the institutions of work, family, and friendship have meanings and uses quite different from the white experience—specifically, in the ghetto these are primarily defense (coping) mechanisms rather than existential experiences. Whyte (1943) and Gans (1962), in their respective participant observations of Italian-American communities in the Boston area, found, much-heightened from white middle-class society, the values of residential stability, kinship, personalized interactions, and a special clinging to traditions from the Old World. Weller (1965), from his perspective of northern minister among southern Appalachians, found that the traits of individualism, traditionalism, fatalism, and personalism combine to form among mountain whites a distinct world view with direct implications for perceptions of government and political behavior generally. And Steiner (1968), following a long line of quasi-participant observers among Indian Americans, notes the centrality of the values of land and ecological harmony in a way which is distinct from the pioneer-homesteading tradition of white society. In sum, the socio-anthropoligical field research on different groups of Americans indicates wide variation in life-style and norms between these groups and any single image of the American national culture.

The relevant question becomes: *how much* diversity is present within the United States—enough to demand group by group analysis of individual political behavior, or not? Are there several distinct political experiences within America, reflecting differing cultural heritages and life-styles, or not?

While it is obvious that Americans differ on measures of phenomena which, in other societies, are often at the root of social conflict—most notably, race, social status, urban-rural residence, religious background, and educational achievement—much of the research on American political behavior seems to say that cleavages on these dimensions somehow "cross-cut," "over-lap," or "melt" at the aggregate level. The balance of this monograph seeks to provide an empirical framework within which this empirical and partly normative debate can be explored.

RESEARCH DESIGN AND METHOD

To test this broad hypothesis about patterns of differences in the political behavior of subgroups in the United States, three groups of Americans were selected for study—Blacks, Appalachians, and Indians. These groups were chosen as three (among many) representatives of minority cultures which have been systematically deprived of an equitable share in the distribution of goods and services by the political system. By nearly all criteria—income, education, health, physical and social mobility, electoral representation, judicial dispositions—these three groups rank very low, though there are variations in individual welfare within the groups. Blacks, Appalachians and Indians, of course, do not represent America—indeed, it is as if they are "non-Americans" in view of their life-outcomes. Rather, the selection of these three groups represents an attempt to test the "cultural reach"—the power of generalization—of extant theories and descriptions of American political behavior.

The formulation of specific hypotheses takes place in two frameworks—methodological and substantive. The methodological framework is concerned with the appropriateness of disaggregating the so-called "national electorate." To return to our earlier argument, at what point (if any) do within-group differences become so great as to render unidimensional summary descriptions of the group (nation) misleading or even meaningless? Is there an American Voter? In order to be able to construct and to generalize on such an entity, we would assert that each of the major subgroups in the society must reflect relatively similar *frequencies* and *patterns* of political attitudes and participation.[5] Otherwise, the American voter or political participant would be a mere statistical artifact—a meaningless average serving only to obscure widely varying distributions and pattern relationships. In specific, then, two hypotheses which derive from this methodological argument are advanced for empirical testing:

(1) each of the three groups (Blacks, Appalachians, Indians) will differ substantially compared with any aggregate national profile of citizen political attitudes and participation, and

(2) each of these three groups will differ among themselves, both with respect to the distributions of political attitudes and participation, and most importantly, with respect to the *correlates* of attitudes and behavior.

If, indeed, cultural diversity and cultural autonomy are goals of Blacks, Appalachians, and Indians (as parts of the social science literature and recent public activities tend to indicate), their reflections in political life will depend upon a complex and *unique* set of interactions with cultural heritage, government contact, and physical setting.

The foregoing hypotheses are extensions of the Przeworski-Teune (1970) framework (method) for studying political phenomena in a comparative or cross-cultural perspective. As such, they do not deal with the substance of political life in the three groups. In a substantive framework, the broadest hypothesis guiding the current investigation suggests that each of these groups, in a parallel but not identical way, will turn to non-electoral styles of political participation as a reflection of the failure of the vote to protect their public status. Thus, it was apparent in the formulation of the research problem that an expanded conceptualization of political participation would be required. Whereas most early observers (Milbrath, 1965; Campbell, 1964; Lane, 1959) and some more recent ones as well (Pomper, 1968) have characterized political behavior exclusively in the imagery of voting and the immediate electoral arena, Lipsky (1970), Keech (1965) and Graham and Gurr (1969) among others have noted the import of activities such as rent-strikes, court litigation, sit-ins, and other forms of protest and media-seeking exposure for pressing demands in the political system, especially for the politically powerless or "out" groups. Other central substantive hypotheses concern the relationship between the circumstances or "context" of individual participative acts and political attitudes, and the distinctiveness or lack of distinctiveness between the concepts of "politics" and "voting" in the mind sets of individuals. These latter two substantive areas of inquiry and potential hypothesis-testing will be explored in some depth for Blacks, Appalachians, and Indians within the framework of an alternative model of political socialization.

Despite these more formal attempts at hypothesis development, however, this work remains partially inductive. At numerous points in the data analysis, elaborate explanations are developed ex post facto where it was not possible from the existing substantive literature on "ethnic groups" to formulate hypothesis in advance. In this sense, then, the work is speculative and raises more hypotheses to be tested (at least in the substantive realm) than it can resolve.

SAMPLING THEORY

After determining that in-depth survey research (face-to-face interviewing) would be the most effective, indeed the only, primary research strategy which could test the foregoing hypotheses, the critical question became: who among these three socially-defined groups is to be sampled? No national sampling of these groups was undertaken, on the grounds that such a procedure would, at the group level, duplicate a misleading methodological assumption of previous research: namely, could any one probability sample describe in any meaningful way Blacks, Appalachians, and Indians? Rather, one different community was selected as a microcosm of each of the cultural groups.

This approach commands several advantages. First, it leaves open for further testing the question of within-group variation: ghetto versus middle-class Blacks, reservation versus urban Indians, improving versus deteriorating Appalachian communities. Other communities can be chosen by other researchers in a (partial) attempt at replication. Secondly, studying one community for each group reduces the distance between observer and observed, a research posture whose value has not been perhaps adequately recognized among methodologists.[6] This approach suggests that the benefits in clarity of interpretation which emerge from personal observation of community life and from utilization of available aggregate data (such as Census data) outweigh any disbenefits resulting from the loss of "objectivity." Nevertheless, it is clear that no single community can reflect the diversity which characterizes even the most homogeneous group. As such, generalizations directed from our samples to the larger cultural experiences in which we are interested must be tentative and limited.

THREE COMMUNITIES[7]

The neighborhood of Venice, within the city of Los Angeles, was chosen as the site for the study of *ghetto* Blacks. A half-century ago Venice was an elegant beach resort; today its central core is a mixed racial-ethnic ghetto—Black, Chicano, and White—with the outer fringes consisting largely of students and street people. Population density is high; so is the drug traffic. Several points which distinguish Venice from some other Black ghettos should be noted here:

(1) While Blacks do form a residential sub-bloc within Venice (from which the actual sample was drawn), they are not isolated physically from the white world.

(2) Venice is not a self-contained political subdivision; its small relative population (20,000) means that it cannot dominate any political jurisdiction; at present, Whites represent Venice at nearly all levels of local public office (except mayor).

(3) Unlike many ghettos, Venice finds itself sandwiched among communities of affluence, on the west side of Los Angeles. Yet on demographic criteria, the marks of ghetto life—low income, high residential mobility, much unemployment and underemployment, deteriorating housing—are all present (see Appendix A for the demographic characteristics of the three samples). Overshadowed by the glare from Watts (about fifteen miles to the east) and lacking in any major disturbances of public order, Venice stands as a severely neglected community.

Claiborne County, Tennessee was chosen as the site for the study of *southern* Appalachian Whites. Situated in the scenic Cumberland Gap of east Tennessee, the county is expansive, mountainous, sparsely populated, and moderately isolated (fifty miles northeast of Knoxville). There are no air or rail links, but a portion of the county does lie along a major secondary road which extends southward from Corbin, Kentucky. Intra-county travel can be lengthy and difficult, as nearly all the major roads run parallel to one another. After a period of steep decline, the population of the county has levelled off (1970: 19,420). Intra-county mobility is increasing as residents abandon shacks in the outlying areas and move toward the county seat. Economically, the life of the county is on the upsurge after the infusion of federal monies in the 1960s from the Appalachian Area Redevelopment Act. Once a mining county, Claiborne is now primarily small farms and small homes. Nevertheless, the level of public services is abysmally low. Law enforcement is severely under-manned; many educational facilities are so dated as to bring howls of protest from the local citizenry; fire protection is nonexistent in some parts of the county; and the lack of solid waste disposal facilities has led to much man-made blight. Politically. the county is administered by a popularly-elected County Judge, as are all counties in Tennessee. Corruption can be widespread in local elections which are almost always hotly contested, and poll-watchers have been known to disappear. In brief, Claiborne County is one of the last of the Appalachian folk counties. Some Appalachian counties will simply wither away; others (probably like Claiborne) will in another generation become Knoxville-suburban.

The Eastern Cherokee Reservation in western North Carolina was chosen as the site for the study of *reservation* Indians.[8] One of two federal reservations east of the Mississippi, the Eastern Cherokee have some 5,000 resident members today. Located at the foot of a scenic national park, the reservation attracts a very large number of tourists from late spring until early autumn. Except for this seasonal economic boom, however, the reservation faces many of the same problems that plague other reserva-tions—poverty, inadequate housing, limited educational and employment opportunities. Politically, the local Bureau of Indian Affairs and the Tribal Band (a legal corporation under the state of North Carolina) dominate the reservation. The B.I.A. remains responsible for the delivery of most primary services on the reservation (education, welfare, roads and transportation, and health through the Public Health Service). The Tribe handles most secondary services (fire protection, sanitation, law enforce-ment). What most sharply distinguishes this tribe from western tribes is the relatively high degree of cultural assimilation to some aspects of the white world among the Eastern Cherokee. Most tribal members speak English fluently, some (especially the young) have never known their native Cherokee tongue. And only a handful of Eastern Cherokee (10 percent) are "full-bloods;" the remainder range down to 1/32 Indian blood (the legal minimum for tribal membership) and perhaps lower in some instances. Within this diversity of heritages, there is an undercurrent of conflict between the "full-bloods" and the "mixed-bloods" on the reservation, manifesting itself among the children in the reservation schools, in the choice of township residence, in occupational patterns, and in tribal elections.

DATA COLLECTION

For sampling within Venice, California, a new housing listing was developed in the field exclusively for this study, and random sampling was employed to locate particular units.[9] In Claiborne County, a general highway map was cross-hatched producing fifteen bloc areas from which six were chosen at random. Within each chosen area, housing units were selected randomly.[10] On the Eastern Cherokee reservation, sampling by housing unit was not possible; instead, two rolls containing the names of all tribal members were utilized for selecting individual respondents at random.[11] In all samples, only adult males were interviewed.[12] With a target goal of sixty interviews in each group, fifty interviews were completed in the Black sample, fifty-eight each in the Appalachian and Indian samples. The interviews, which ranged from forty minutes to several hours in length, were conducted in staggered sequences from September 1970 through March 1971, a period of much turmoil in American political life. In Venice, interviewing was conducted exclusively by Black male residents of that ghetto; on the Eastern Cherokee reservation, exclusively by male tribal members; in Claiborne County, both by the author and local male residents.[13]

AN ALTERNATIVE MODEL OF POLITICAL SOCIALIZATION

Essentially, three major categories of data emerge from our interviews:

(1) personal background data
(2) information on the frequency and circumstances (context) of political participation
(3) data on political attitudes (collapsed through scale construction).

A political socialization framework has been chosen for integrating these categories of data and for providing an additional theoretical mosaic within which hypotheses regarding within-nation differences are to be tested.

Figure 1 illustrates a dynamic or developmental view of the socialization process, beginning with personal background and extending through a continuous interplay between political life-experiences and attitudes. In brief, it is posited that the political experiences which people have as adults—both their frequency and the "context" in which they occur—are intermediary socializing forces in the development of attitudes about

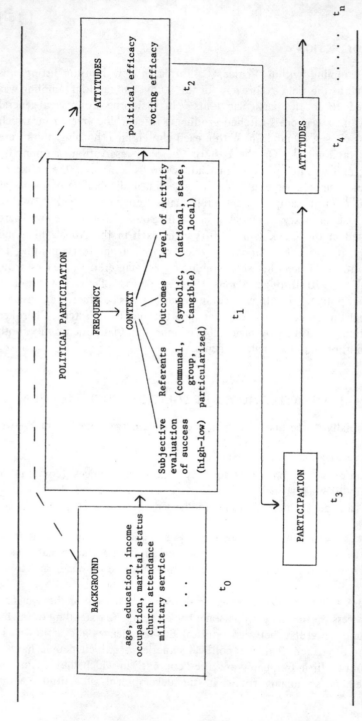

Figure 1: A DYNAMIC MODEL OF POLITICAL SOCIALIZATION: THE IMPACT OF ADULT POLITICAL EXPERIENCES

government, politics, and one's role in the political community. Such a theory stands in contrast to the predominant model of political socialization in which childhood experiences (family, school, peer group) are viewed as the sole or primary socializing agents (Hess and Torney, 1967; Greenstein, 1965; Hyman, 1959). Nonetheless, there have been some recent theoretical speculations and supportive empirical findings for the role of adult experiences (Jennings and Niemi, 1973; Searing, 1973; Jacob, 1969; Brim and Wheeler, 1966).

Equally, our model of socialization seems the only methodologically defensible one, given the cross-sectional nature of our data-gathering. While some researchers have utilized attitudes measured at the time of the interview to *predict* behaviors which necessarily occurred before the interview (and, therefore, before the "attitudes" themselves), Nie (1970) cautions theoretical and statistical model-builders to include only "logically prior variables" as independent variables in regression analysis, a warning which seems very well founded.

In sum, we are arguing for the empirical existence (or at least possibility) of an open and changeable political personality—one which responds not only to the stimuli of parental and childhood appendages, but to adult political experiences, routine as well as extraordinary. Further, attitudes cannot be viewed as an end-point any more than participation. As our model indicates, we perceive a constant interchange between behavior and attitudes throughout an individual's life, though the intensity of the interchanges may be diminished somewhat at later stages in adulthood. In the sections following, we will provide data and comment on one slice of the developmental model.

PARTICIPATION OPERATIONALIZED

In this research, extensive data were gathered on both "electoral" and "non-electoral" political activities for each of the three cultural groups. The electoral activities paralleled Milbrath's (1965) early conceptualization: wearing buttons, writing letters, attending rallies, etc. Non-electoral participation included such activities as ad hoc interest group activity ("involved in local public issue"), participation in ongoing community or civic organizations, economic boycotts, picketing, demonstrations, and protests. Wording for some of these non-electoral activities was decentralized to take into account the varying physical settings in which our three samples were located. In all, a total of thirteen categories (seven electoral, six non-electoral) comprised the two styles of political participation. Inevitably, any sampling of political activities is somewhat arbitrary even in the presence of theoretical guidelines, for a slightly different range of activities would result in different frequencies of participation. Further, the selection task becomes more difficult in a cross-cultural study where the goal is to sample a representative range of political options in each of the cultural groups. Given the seemingly broad wording of actual questions and the intensive probing by the interviewers, however, the severity of this problem should be reduced.

Table 1 presents the frequency distributions for participation in the various kinds of activities. In each instance, respondents were asked to recall whether *ever in their lifetime* they had engaged in a given political act. This represents some departure from previous research where it has been common practice to inquire about participation in a relatively restricted period of time (often a presidential election campaign.)[14] It is this researcher's belief that a wider time frame affords a better perspective for studying the character and rate of participation, in part because of the expanded conceptualization of participation to include non-electoral activities.

Table 1 indicates that these are activities common to large numbers of Blacks and Appalachians, but small numbers of Indians. Only two activities (personal contact and ad hoc issue activity) have touched the lives of more than a fourth of the Indian sample, whereas seven or more activities have permeated at least 25 percent of the Black and Appalachian samples. While Indians clearly rank the lowest in participation in most activities, similarities exist in the frequencies of the other two groups, although Blacks have participated somewhat more frequently in most non-electoral activities whereas Appalachians have participated somewhat more frequently in most electoral activities. In part, because information on the number of repetitions of political activities could not feasibly be gathered, the data represent (more accurately) *diversity* in political participation.

Initially, electoral and non-electoral activities were conceptualized to be two distinctive styles or "modes" of political participation. However, such a distinction proved slippery at the conceptual level: at what point do "rallies" and "meetings" turn into "riots" and "demonstrations?" The problem also occurs at the empirical level (moderately high correlation between the frequency of electoral and non-electoral activities in each of the samples; $r = .58$ among Blacks, $r = .42$ among Appalachians, $r = .61$ among Indians). Political activism is a sufficiently generalized phenomenon that it transcends simple classifications such as electoral/non-electoral. The population of participants does not depend very much on the "electoral-relatedness" or "conventionality" of the political act, at least in our data.

TABLE 1
Frequency Distributions for Electoral and Non-Electoral Participation

(Percentage of Respondents Reporting Having Participated in a
Specific Political Activity at Least Once in their Lifetime)

	BLACK	APPALACHIAN	INDIAN
ELECTORAL			
Wear button/display sticker or sign	50.0%	55.2%	8.8%
Write letter to political figure	28.0	37.9	12.3
Talk personally with political figure	22.0	50.0	38.6
Contribute money to political campaign/cause	26.0	25.9	5.3
Attend political meeting/rally	50.0	67.2	15.8
Work in election campaign	16.0	37.9	8.8
Run for political office	4.0	10.3	14.0
CPA[a]	.483	.500	.586
NON-ELECTORAL			
Be involved in local public issue	28.0	51.7	27.6
Participate in community organization	34.7	17.2	12.1
Boycott store or business	38.0	20.7	12.1
Picketing	22.4	3.4	0.0
Participate in protest/demonstration	30.6	12.1	0.0
Do anything else political (misc.)	12.2	1.7	0.0
CPA[a]	.601	.415	.667
N	(50)	(58)	(58)

a. CPA refers to "Concentration of Political Activism" Index; the CPA Index is a modification of Alker's "normalized mean deviation" designed to measure the relative concentration or dispersion of political activism for a given sample. The modified statistic has an effective range from 0 to 1; the higher the score, the more concentrated the degree of activism among a (relatively) few individuals in a sample. For a brief discussion of the normalized mean deviation, see Alker (1965: 39-40).

Accordingly, we have confidence in the reliability and validity of a measure of political participation which incorporates both electoral and non-electoral activities. Others (Verba, 1971) have been able to demonstrate, however tenuously, distinct clusters of political activities. Rather than searching further for these, however, we intend to pursue a new path—to differentiate political participation according to the *context* or circumstances under which it takes place.

THE CONTEXT OF PARTICIPATION

Political participation has been analyzed almost exclusively in a quantitative framework—how often (if at all) does a given individual participate in various activities? However, political participation is not only a set of activities in which people engage, but a set of *experiences* which people have. One may have lots of political experiences or few; equally important for those who do participate, individuals may have qualitatively different kinds of experience—by level (national, state, local), by motivation (on behalf of which individuals, for what purpose), and by result (successful or unsuccessful). What then are the circumstances which surround and give meaning to the frequency with which one participates in the political system? Three dimensions of the context of participation, which are susceptible to operationalization, will be explored in some depth.

At What Level?

One important part of the context of participation involves the level at which an individual enters the political arena. Not only do the structures of political life differ at national, state, and local levels, but potentially so do the resultant images and perceptions of politics among participants. Interacting with a local bureaucracy whose roots lie in personal power and patronage and whose processes may display overt corruption is quite different from contact with a highly professional, depersonalized, federal bureaucracy. Chatting with a U.S. Senator or agency director affords a different vision of the workings of politics than arguing with the local school board superintendent. National politics is often abstract and lofty; local politics is the concrete crossroad where public services must intersect individual citizens. National politicians can "deliver" by voting the right way or saying the right thing; it is local officials who typically bear the burden of converting the expenditures of government into things people value—education, safety, justice, leisure.

In our data, it was possible to distinguish beyond simply national versus local experience. For *electoral* activities, five levels were delineated for the Black and Appalachian samples, six for the Indian sample—Presidential, U.S. Senatorial, Congressional, Statewide, Local (and Tribal). For non-electoral activities, it was not possible to determine level. For example, while it is clear what level "working in a congressional election campaign" represents (Congressional), it is highly ambiguous what level is represented by picketing Sears Roebuck, boycotting grapes, or attending a demonstration in supoort of Angela Davis. When the focus shifts away from electoral pressure points to the distribution of values (as in non-electoral activities), level becomes much less distinguishable. Thus, the context variable "level of political activity" will refer only to *electoral* political activities in the distribution presented in Table 2 and in subsequent analytic manipulations.

Table 2 reveals some interesting differences in the "level-emphasis" of participation among the three groups,[15] but perhaps the most important point to be drawn from the table is the nature of the absolute frequencies of participation at the various levels. Much political research has focused on participation at the highest levels, but for a variety of ideological and methodological reasons, fewer studies have tapped local activism.[16] It is clear from the above data that local (electoral-related) experiences are quite frequent for all three cultural groups, though the meaning of "local" differs according to the physical settings in which the groups are located, a point to be discussed more fully later. Indeed, local participation is more frequent in all three groups (in varying degree) than presidential-level participation. Local political activities may or may not be so experientially intense or attitudinally-significant as higher-level activities, but the very frequency with which they occur (including the act of voting itself)[17] suggests that they merit further study. In addition to ignoring non-electoral political experiences, the classic political participation studies have seemingly tapped only a small segment of the *level-range* of electoral political experiences.

Why?

Most researchers have chosen to search for the demographic roots of participation in attempting to answer the question: "Why do people come to get involved in politics?" Although such background characteristics may partially explain whether people will or will not participate generally, it is difficult to link them with an individual's inclination to take part in any *specific* political act. No single motivation indiscriminately accounts for all

TABLE 2
Distribution of Electoral Political Experiences
by Level of Activity

	BLACK	APPALACHIAN	INDIAN
PRESIDENTIAL	29.8%	16.0%	3.8%
U.S. SENATORIAL	12.3	13.4	5.6
CONGRESSIONAL	5.2	18.7	30.2
STATEWIDE	14.1	12.7	5.6
LOCAL	38.6	39.2	19.0
TRIBAL	--	--	35.8
	100.0%	100.0%	100.0%
N^a	(103)	(178)	(63)

a. Missing data have been excluded from calculations of percentages.

political behavior for any one individual; different motivations push people at various times and for various types of activities. Indeed, as Lane (1959) thoughtfully points out, not all goals for political activity can even be articulated at a conscious level; some need be found deep in one's psyche. Since survey research can only record what an individual says were his reasons for participating, we must be content at most with conscious motivations. Drawing on the (Verba, 1971) two-dimensional framework for analyzing the potential gratifications which an individual might receive from participation, two sub-dimensions identifying an individual's *motivations* for political acts will be presented—"referent" and "outcome."

The referent sub-dimension concerns the scope of individuals on whose behalf a person participates in a given political act. In other words, how broad a referent does an individual invoke for why he took part in the act? The roots of some political experiences may be phrased in *communal* terms (a collectivity—the community, society, mankind), others in *group* terms (a physical or psychological group—farmers, union members, Blacks, Indians), still others in *particularized* terms (individual *qua* individual—family, friends, self).

The outcome sub-dimension refers to the nature of the goal which one seeks from participation. If "for whom" is the relevant question for referent, "for what kind of purpose" is the parallel question for outcome. Does the individual articulate motivations in terms of *symbolic* outcomes (broad, unlimited, undefined—making the world safe for democracy, justice for Blacks, a sense of personal security) or *tangible* outcomes (narrow, defined, limited—elimination of air pollution, collective bargaining for workers, job for self or family member)? As the examples seek to illustrate, the referent and outcome sub-dimensions are at least conceptually independent of one another.

Before summarizing the relevant frequency distributions, it should be noted that considerable and unambiguous detail about a given experience was required before it could be coded on the referent and outcome categories; in a sizeable percentage of instances, such detail and clarity were lacking. Further, some political activity engages the participant as passive object or victim (accidentally stumbling into a political figure and briefly talking with him) where there really is no prior goal or motivation for participation, conscious or unconscious. Thus, while both electoral and non-electoral experiences were coded for these two sub-dimensions, the overall number of political experiences on which the dimensions are based is considerably reduced.

The frequency proportions for communal, group, and particularized referents were not greatly different from one another across our samples of Blacks, Appalachians, and Indians, but for each group the *modal* referent was different. For Blacks, experiences were most likely to be articulated in group terms (42%), reflecting the special salience of racial identity. For Indians, communal referents were most frequent (45%), reflecting reservation-wide concerns (self-contained collectivity of Whites and Indians rather than Pan-Indianism per se.) For Appalachians, particularized referents were most frequent (45%), providing support for Weller's (1965) field observation that the mountain white's "individualism and person-orientation team up to lead him into politics so that he can get favors for his own area, people, and reference group."

The frequency proportions for symbolic and tangible outcomes were very similar across our three samples. In each case, tangible outcomes were articulated almost twice as frequently as symbolic outcomes.

With What Success?

Perhaps the most important dimension of one's political experiences is the "success" (or lack of) which accompanies them. But what constitutes a successful experience? Much of the participation literature has focused on the *efficacy* of individual action—the chance to affect public policy and decision-making. While this undoubtedly is an important element, Lane (1959) and Hoffer (1951) among others suggest that it is not the only one. For example, Edelman (1964) argues that a sense of enjoyment or involvement, a chance to express one's positive and negative energies are the best results which people can realistically come to expect from political participation. While in one sense that may understate the significance of other elements, the *emotions* which an experience generates would seem to play a part in the evaluation which an individual consciously or unconsciously makes. Still a third element might be the *personal feedback* which an individual gets from participating—does he make new friends or new enemies? Does he get a new job or get busted? In the overall perspective, these three elements would seem to be among the most important in the matrix of individual perceptions of success. Of course, they may not be equally salient for each individual; people differ not only in the proximate motivations which lead them to participate in a specific act but in the deeper motivations which affect their general inclination to participate or not to participate. For some, perhaps, emotional involvement may be most important; for others, influencing policy or receiving personal benefits (physical or psychological). Given the lack of refinement which survey research offers in this area, we have chosen to construct a Success Index for each individual based on an *equal* weighting of the three elements, nevertheless recognizing the inherent weaknesses in such an assumption. Figure 2 displays the numeric coding operationalization of the Success Index.

In brief, it can be noted that most political experiences in each of the three groups were reported to be moderately favorable. The emotion and feedback elements were most consistently reported to be sources of

		Success Level	
	3	2	1
Element	HIGH	MEDIUM	LOW
EMOTION	Positive	Indifferent Other Not Ascertained	Negative
EFFICACY	Efficacious	Uncertain Not Ascertained	Inefficacious
FEEDBACK	Benefit	No Feedback Uncertain Not Ascertained	Harm
OVERALL SCORE	9	6	3

Figure 2: Construction of "Success Index" for a Political Experience

satisfaction (experience success); among Appalachians and Indians, virtually no harmful feedback or negative personal emotions were reported as parts of specific political experiences recalled to the interviewer, though a few such cases appeared among Blacks. With respect to efficacy, however, approximately one-third of all experiences in each group were perceived by the participant as inefficacious.

Discussion of the "context" of participation, although lengthy, has served to introduce a new set of variables into the study of political participation. In this particular research, these variables were hypothesized to play an important role in explaining the generation and modification of political attitudes such as political efficacy and voting efficacy, topics to be discussed at some length in subsequent data analysis sections.

THE ORIGINS OF PARTICIPATION

While the primary emphasis in this research places political participation in a socialization framework—intervening between early childhood experiences and later political attitudes—it would seem helpful at the outset of data analysis to examine what kinds of people in each of our three groups have greater or lessened chances to reach a frequent participative stage. From the broader view of the distribution of public goods and services, participation itself can be seen to be positively valued in that many services come only to those who actively seek them (welfare benefits, food stamps, recreational facilities). Thus, for the moment we are asking: who gets this intermediary value—who gets his day in the "political sun?" Such a perspective may differ from others who have sought to explain the phenomenon of participation in that participation is seen here as a value to be obtained and personal background as the arena where forces of exclusion interact; participation has more often been viewed as an inherently equal-opportunity decision in which inequality results from influences which are psychological rather than political and, therefore, ones which the individual can himself ultimately control (Milbrath, 1965; Lane, 1959; Rosenberg, 1955). But the individual's childhood appendages are much like original sin—beyond the control of any one individual. The skills and resources which participation demands are not equally available to all citizens. The distribution of other values (education, wealth, justice) sharply affects an individual's chance of participating.

Some may perceive that we are herein locked in the "demographic determinism" versus "free will" debate. But that discussion misses an important point, *the* point in fact: the systematically inequitable distribution of public goods and services. In the language of organic political systems, it is the outputs of the system which generate and shape the nature of the inputs, as much as the reverse.

DATA ANALYSIS

Our analysis of data begins with an examination of the origins of participation as derived from stepwise multiple regressions performed *separately* for each of the three groups. For each group, the dependent variable is an interval measure of the frequency/diversity of political participation; its value can range from zero to thirteen, depending upon the number of different kinds of electoral-related and non-electoral political activities in which an individual has engaged in the course of his lifetime.[18] At this point in the analysis, the "logically prior" independent variables are personal background variables as indicated in Figure I and operationalized in Appendix B. Thus, we are asking which variables account for differences in levels of individual political participation within each of the three samples, once tests for multicollinearity have established the (relative) statistical independence of the predictor variables.[19] Do the same variables emerge for each group, or do different pattern interrelationships appear? Table 3 reports the beta weights (standardized regression coefficients) as well as the zero-order correlation coefficients for the statistically significant predictors which emerged for each group from separate stepwise multiple regressions on the number of different kinds of political experiences; also reported are the multiple correlation coefficients (R) for the significant predictors taken together.

Table 3 reveals that the elements in an individual's personal background which lead toward or away from political participation *vary* by group, and in some instances the directional impact of certain background characteristics is reversed. Within the Black sample, note that a high educational level relative to other Blacks in the sample, a low income compared with others in the sample, and not attending church "regularly" are the significant independent predictors of frequent political participation. The respective beta weights indicate that education is the single most important predictor in the Black sample. Within the Appalachian sample, two variables—income and age—are significant predictors of political participation. But it is a high relative income which leads to political activity for Appalachians, *reversed* from the Black sample. Being older also predicts, but much less so, to political activity for the Appalachian sample. Within the Indian sample, a more complex pattern of participation emerges; six background variables are significant predictors of political activity. Like Appalachians, having a high relative income and being older predict to

TABLE 3
Stepwise Multiple Regression — Predictors of Electoral and
Non-Electoral Participation: The Influence of Personal Background

	BLACK		APPALACHIAN		INDIAN	
	beta	(r)	beta	(r)	beta	(r)
Predictors						
INCOME	−.31	(−.23)	.56	(.53)	.30	(.50)
AGE	---		.24	(.15)	.25	(.25)
CHURCH ATTENDANCE	−.21	(−.34)	---		.19	(.28)
EDUCATION	.45	(.42)	---		---	
LOCATION OF SCHOOLING[a]	---		---		.27	(.52)
NUMBER OF CHILDREN	x[c]		---		−.20	(−.27)
REDNESS	x[c]		x[c]		−.17	(−.23)
MULTIPLE R	.58**		.58***		.70**	
N[b]	(50)		(58)		(58)	

a. In testing for multicollinearity, location of schooling was combined with birthplace for the Black and Appalachian samples, but the resultant variable did not emerge as a significant predictor in either group.
b. Pairwise deletion was utilized for missing data.
c. Data on this variable not collected for a given sample.
  ** Regression equation statistically significant at .01.
*** Regression equation statistically significant at .001.

more frequent activity; so also do attending church "regularly" (reversed from the Black sample), having attended school *off* the reservation, having fewer children, and having a lower degree of "Redness" (a variable which combines in equal weighting the language which an individual speaks and the blood degree of Indian ancestry). The beta weights indicate that these six variables are not substantially different in the independent contribution which each makes. For all three samples, it is also important to note that in each instance the zero-order correlation between the predictor variable and participation parallels the *direction* of impact suggested by the beta.

Having presented a summary of the origins of political participation in each group, let us now turn to the analysis of theoretical links. Two background variables operate in differing directions vis-a-vis participation in the three groups—church attendance and income. Why?

Regular church attendance is a depressant to political activity for Blacks while it is a positive contributor for Indians. Turning to the level of system, one possible explanation might be that the ideology and functions of the church as an institution differ for Blacks and Indians.[20] For Black Americans, Marx's characterization of religion as the "opiate of the masses" may be partially relevant. While most churches in the society generally tend to emphasize "otherworldliness" at the expense of the present, the special functions of the ghetto church and the low status of Blacks as a group may provide the specific conditions under which the ideological message of religious fervor for the future has its greatest impact. As Kenneth Clark (1965) notes, the ghetto church (in Harlem) provides a place for social togetherness and emotional release—perhaps the only such place in the "pathology" of ghetto life. Similarly, Dixon and Foster (1971) point out that organized religion in the ghetto has been a source of "sustenance" and "fulfillment." Thus, despite the church's role as an avenue for the recruitment of political *leaders* in the ghetto, for ordinary Black citizens the church may divert attention away from the inequities and injustices of public life. While most in our sample are not regular church-goers (by their own definitions of "regular"), this institution seems to have a substantial residual impact on its relatively small clientele. For Indians, in contrast, the church in a way not unlike pot-luck suppers or athletic contests on the reservation may be a vehicle for the kind of group activity which emphasizes outwardness and social interaction. Referring to the "non-religious" functions which the church appears to fill specifically on the Eastern Cherokee reservation, Kutsche (1961) asks:

> The question remains, to what extent the Christian church in Big Cove [one of the six townships on the Eastern Cherokee reservation] fills a religious function at all, if we employ the definition of religion as belief and practice concerning the supernatural.

While Kutsche's conceptualization of religion may be narrow, the point is clear: church-going on the reservation can be interpreted as public activity which brings people in contact with others, and which may play a role in mobilizing more explicitly political activities amidst a privatization ethos of reservation Indian life (Ryan, 1972b).

The second reversal between background variables and participation occurs with family income. For all three groups, income is a significant predictor of the dependent variable, participation—but in a negative direction for Blacks, while in a positive direction for Appalachians and Indians. In most previous research, income has been hypothesized and found to have a positive association with frequency of political activity. From a theoretical perspective, it is argued that having a relatively high income enables individuals to spend less time worrying about physical survival, leaving more time for leisure activities, one of which is politics. Further, a higher income typically provides easier access to public officials as well as a commodity for bargaining or extracting political favor and influence. These would seem to be highly plausible theoretical linkages for the positive associations within our Appalachian and Indian samples. For Blacks, however, clearly a different explanation is required since the directionality of the relationship between the two variables is reversed. It may be that in the ghetto having a relatively high income leads to a network of middle-class (bourgeois) relationships in which the individual seeks stability and influence through the most legitimated political channel—voting, but not through other political activities which might bring him into close contact with the militants.[21] Equally, a relatively low income in the ghetto may sometimes reflect marginal or part-time working status which would free the individual to concentrate on political activity. Our findings and interpretations here seem consonant with those of the National Advisory Commission on Civil Disorders of 1968. In interesting ways, our profile of the Black political activist parallels that of the Commission's "rioter."

The differing influence of income as an independent variable in the three samples indirectly points to another related difference: the relationship between income and education in the three samples. As independent variables which would normally be expected to be highly intercorrelated (as indicators of social status), the inclusion of income and education in multiple regression analysis would present a serious methodological obstacle. The spectre of multicollinearity (if too large) can render an analysis meaningless. In our data, the problem was vexing, yet of conceptual and substantive interest. Education and (family) income are moderately correlated in our Appalachian ($r = .48$) and Indian ($r = .43$) samples, but only very slightly related in our Black sample ($r = .24$). Though there are some methodological artifacts which could be at play,[22] a substantive interpretation is at least equally compelling. Some might immediately interpret the low correlation in the Black sample as evidence of racial discrimination (for which there already exists related kinds of quantitative documentation). However, given the nature of the Venice community and its residents, the most convincing explanation seems to relate to the meaning of the concept of social status itself. Education and income represent two different life-styles in Venice (and perhaps in other Black ghettos): relatively high income but low education represents the middle-aged or older migrant from the South, holding down a reasonably stable, if unexciting, job in Los Angeles with little time or psychic life-energies left over for politics (except voting); whereas the obverse— high education (some college) and low income, represents the Los Angeles-born young hip-activist black who sees and *pursues* the need for non-traditional styles of political intervention. Such an analysis rests in part on an observational "understanding" of the Venice community, but is also confirmed by preliminary factor analyses undertaken for other purposes. A careful look at Appendix D will reveal that both Factors 1 and 2 in the Black sample reflect the "militant" versus "Uncle Tom" dichotomy. In Factor 1, the participation nexus consists of higher education, younger age, not being married, and having been born and educated outside the South. In Factor 2, the voting core is linked in exactly the opposite direction with most of those background variables. In sum, education and income represent two (involuntary?) paths to different kinds of "status" in this Black community, in ways which are not true for the Appalachian and Indian samples.

Several other relationships which appear in Table 3 deserve some theoretical elaboration.[23] The meaning of the variable "age" has been a slippery one in political research.[24] It can either mean the influence of life-style or of the historical period in which an individual grew up. Also, in our data the positive association between age and participation may simply reflect the particular time-span of inquiry (lifetime) and the natural potential for the accumulation of many different kinds of political experiences over the course of many years. However, in view of the large percentage of activities which were reported to have occurred within the last two or four years (preceding the interview) in all samples, it seems likely that the relationship is not mere artifact.[25] For Indians, old age seems to be revered in ways very much unlike white, middle-class society. Whereas most of America sends its aged off to institutions, Indians often invest the highest authority in their aged. The personification of wisdom, the Chief, has often been an old man in Indian history and folklore. Thus, it may be expected that younger men will at least refrain from seeking political *leadership* roles, especially on rural reservations such as the Eastern Cherokee where few young men are being trained in the universities despite a large increase in college-educated youth in the society at-large.[26] Without a young, educated elite, the accumulation of knowledge through living seems the surest path to the wisdom which tribes have historically expected of their political leaders and activists.

The remaining background variables which predict to participation in the Indian sample also deserve brief theoretical note. Attending school *off* the Reservation (that is, in Oklahoma or the Southwest) may provide a young man with an opportunity for expanded social perspective, something essential for receptivity to future political activity. Raising fewer children allows people more free time and indirectly, more money, both of which are supportive of higher participation rates in general (though it is not clear why this should apply to the Indian sample but not to Appalachians).[27] The negative relationship between Redness and participation is somewhat less obvious. Perhaps it is a "value-systems" conflict; politics may be perceived as a "white man's activity." This interpretation receives some support when the relationship is broken down by level of political activity. At the tribal level, there is no relationship between the two variables—Indians high on Redness are neither more nor less likely than Indians low on Redness to participate in reservation politics. In non-tribal political activities, however, Indians high on Redness are much *less* likely to participate.

Finally, the multiple correlation coefficients (R) indicate that variation in the frequency of individual political participation is more "completely" explained for the Indian sample than for Blacks or Appalachians. Almost 50 percent of the variation in participation is accounted for by the set of predictors among Indians, while only about 35 percent of the variance in Black and Appalachian participation rates is accounted for by their respective sets of predictors.[28] However, it is clear that for all three groups a substantial portion of the variance remains unaccounted for by personal background variables. In short, the origins of participation lie beyond any simple interplay of background forces. Other, more proximate, elements which we are unable to quantify (and perhaps even conceptualize) must also explain some of these differences among individuals within each sample. Finally, the *patterns* of interrelationship differ by group; "systems differ" markedly. In many respects, this hardly seems surprising. Yet we have been able to identify the substantive ways in which the origins of participation differ for each of our samples and to suggest at times *system-level* variables (such as the church) in the search for theoretical explanations of these differences.

FINDINGS: THE IMPACT OF PARTICIPATION

Having presented a preliminary view of the nature of political participation among Blacks, Appalachians, and Indians, we turn to resolve the central questions of this research: in what ways and how much do the experiences which people have in politics affect their subsequent attitudes? In other words, once individuals arrive at a participative stage (however minimal), what difference does it make? Are the outcomes uniform or selective by group?

In this section, we will be concerned with two specific attitude constructs—"political efficacy" and "voting efficacy." Political efficacy is defined as the degree to which an individual feels he can influence the political system *at various levels and through diverse modes* of political action. Voting efficacy refers to the degree to which an individual feels he can influence the political system *primarily or exclusively through voting.* It was hypothesized that these would be two separate and distinct "attitudes" in each of the three groups. In contrast, the traditional SRC political efficacy scale tends to equate political efficacy with voting efficacy by operationalizing political efficacy primarily through statements which ask individuals to assess their effectiveness through voting and elections.[29] To search for these attitudes, then, factor analyses were performed on an identical pool of Likert-type attitude items separately for each of the groups. While an extensive explanation of the procedure utilized is beyond the scope of this monograph,[30] two points should be made:

(1) the emergent scales designed to represent the two attitude constructs contained some items which were common to all three groups as well as other items which were not (see Appendix F), providing further evidence through the *structure* of attitudes that "systems differ," and

(2) the scales themselves were derived from a psychometric (simple additive) rather than factor score model.

To return briefly to our developmental model of political socialization, both the frequency and the context of political activities are hypothesized to have independent effects on political attitudes (that is, political efficacy, voting efficacy), beyond the impact of personal background variables.

The empirical thrust of the participation literature in concert with its normative undercurrents suggests that relatively frequent participation leads to more supportive or efficacious political attitudes. Yet that assumes the political system to be benevolent, therein providing participants with positive experiences. While we can offer no intersubjective evidence on system benevolence in general, our data do indicate that all political experiences are not equally successful and that some are downright unhappy ones. Accordingly, we have specified the context of participation, not for descriptive purposes but for theoretically-linked uses in our socialization model. Even when crudely measured (as with the Success Index), one might hypothesize that individuals with successful political experiences in the past would be more politically efficacious in their present attitudes than those with less successful experiences.

With respect to the level at which an individual enters the (electoral) political arena, one might hypothesize that *local* political activity would more readily lead to efficacious political attitudes because such activity is physically more proximate to the individual participant and, therefore, more understandable. Alternatively, one might counter-hypothesize that the type of impact resulting from local political activity would be dependent upon the varying nature of local political establishments. Local communities can be expected to differ on system benevolence; experiences with relatively impermeable or corrupt systems might result in less efficacious political attitudes.

Finally, to hypothesize directionality for the "why" of participation is most difficult. It might be that participating in politics for a communal referent or symbolic outcome would create inflated expectations which could not easily be met, resulting in less efficacious attitudes. Alternatively, it might be that because broad referents and abstract outcomes are less situation-specific, it is these which will lead to more efficacy because one can more easily rationalize (distort) failure into success. For example, if one enters politics to get a job for family or friend, the result is rather clear-cut—one either gets the job or not; whereas if one enters politics to make the community "a better place to live" or to restore "ecological balance" to the universe, the result of individual action becomes more ambiguous and perhaps more subject to distortion.[31]

While the foregoing remarks might seem to suggest identical linkages between the several participation variables (frequency, context) and political versus voting efficacy, that is not the intent. If political efficacy and voting efficacy are, indeed, distinct attitudinal sets, their correlates must also differ—if we are to extend the Przeworski-Teune (1970) logic. However, given the lack of prior research in exploring the possible distinction between politics and voting, our research must again fall back on an inductive path and await the light of data.

Several other technical notes must be offered, however, before proceeding to the testing of these hypotheses. In the stepwise multiple regression analyses to be presented, several independent variables not yet introduced have also been included. One such variable is a composite index of voting frequency—weighting equally, voting in national and local elections where these indicators themselves were correlated. (The act of voting itself was *not* part of the thirteen political activities on which the earlier regression was run, nor was it an activity for which data on its "context" could be collected.) Secondly, voluntary group memberships were theorized to be a significant type of adult political socializing experience. In actuality, for Appalachians and Indians the number of such memberships was highly interrelated with the frequency of electoral and non-electoral participation, and, therefore, was dropped. However, membership in one specific organization (the Farm Bureau) was retained in the Appalachian sample because it proved empirically distinct from the participation cluster (see Appendix D).

Finally, a serious analytic problem was posed by the high rate of non-participation in our Indian sample. Because almost half (41 percent) of the sample reported no political experiences beyond voting, our measures of the context of participation would contain so many missing observations that their exclusion would seem required. Yet for those Indians who do participate, these contextual measures might be important in explaining political attitudes. The most useful solution to this problem seemed to be to divide the Indian sample into two subgroups—"participants" versus "non-participants." In this way, all theoretically-linked variables could be taken into account for each subgroup. Accordingly, however, the subsamples are quite small, and the resultant stepwise regression results are less stable.

POLITICAL EFFICACY

Stepwise multiple regression analyses were performed on political efficacy scale scores separately for each group. For an exact list of the independent variables included for each group, the reader is referred to Appendix E. Table 4 reports the beta weights as well as zero-order correlation coefficients for the statistically significant predictors of political efficacy which emerged for each of the groups, as well as the multiple correlation coefficients (R) for the significant predictors taken together.

An overview of Table 4 reveals several broad findings:

(1) Participation variables do emerge as significant predictors for Blacks, Appalachians, and "participating" Indians. But it is not the frequency of electoral/non-electoral participation which is significant; it is the *contextual* aspects of political experience which are linked with political efficacy.

(2) Although some background variables do have a residual impact on political efficacy, neither education nor age—variables often associated with efficacy in past studies (Bennett and Klecka, 1970;

TABLE 4
Stepwise Multiple Regression: Predictors of
High Political Efficacy

Predictors	BLACK beta	(r)	APPALACHIAN beta	(r)	INDIAN PARTICIPANTS beta	(r)	INDIAN NON-PARTICIPANTS beta	(r)
PARTICIPATION VARIABLES								
FEELINGS OF SUCCESS	---		.39	(.39)	.42	(.26)	x^d	
% LOCAL EXPERIENCES[a]	.29	(.37)	-.23	(-.24)	-.28	(-.18)	x^d	
% COMMUNAL REFERENTS	-.36	(-.24)	---		---		x^d	
VOTING FREQUENCY	---		---		---		$.36^b$	(.54)
BACKGROUND VARIABLES								
INCOME	---		$.23^d$	(.38)	---		---	
EMPLOYMENT STATUS	---		x^d		-.37	(-.27)	---	
OCCUPATION TYPE (FARM)	x^d		-.23	(-.32)	x^d		x^d	
CHURCH ATTENDANCE	$.45^d$	(.50)	---		---		---	
REDNESS	x^d		x^d		---		.38	(.55)
MULTIPLE R	.65**		.61**		.51		.64*	
N[c]	(50)		(58)		(34)		(24)	

a. For Indians, "local" experiences include both tribal and county political activities; for Blacks and Appalachians, county or below.
b. Includes voting in non-tribal elections only; see factor analysis for Indian sample in Appendix D.
c. Pairwise deletion was utilized for missing data.
d. Data on this variable not collected for a given sample. (Note: In the Appalachian sample, employment status—working v. non-working—reflected insufficient variation for analysis).
* Regression equation statistically significant at .05.
** Regression equation statistically significant at .01.

Milbrath, 1965; Almond and Verba, 1963)—emerges significant for any of the groups.

(3) The groups reflect somewhat different predictors of political efficacy; only one variable—the percentage of total political experiences which occurred at the local level—remains in the regression equation for all groups, and its direction of relationship is reversed in the Black sample compared with Appalachians and participating Indians.

(4) The multiple R is moderately high for all groups, though for participating Indians the coefficient is lower and fails to meet accepted levels of statistical significance. On the whole, however, the multiple correlation coefficients are sufficiently high that analysis of individual predictors is meaningful.

Let us begin specific interpretation of Table 4 by reviewing first the impact of local political activity for all three participant groups. That the relationship between local experiences and political efficacy differs by group suggests that one possible hypothesis—closer, more proximate/ personal experiences lead to greater feelings of efficacy—must be rejected. Such an explanation should logically apply uniformly across all groups; in addition, if anything, Blacks' local experiences are the least "local" by that conceptualization of the variable. While Claiborne County and the Eastern Cherokee reservation necessarily reflect the personalization of politics because of limited populations, that is not true for the greater Los Angeles area (county or city).[32] Rather, it would seem that the nature and characteristics of the local political system—such as the degree of responsiveness to public demands, honesty, efficiency—affect subsequent evaluations of personal political effectiveness.[33] For Blacks, Los Angeles-Venice takes on the face of a "benign" system, perhaps because it is a decentralized system not dominated by machine politics. In contrast, patronage, nepotism, corruption, and factionalism continue to be an integral part of local politics in the southern mountains of Tennessee and North Carolina. That such styles of politics fail to generate feelings of great power or influence among citizens on the outside is hardly surprising.

Now, let us return to our samples individually for the remainder of the analysis of Table 4. Among Blacks, two other variables are significant predictors of political efficacy—regular church attendance, and entrance into the political arena on behalf of narrow referents (family or oneself) rather than communal referents (mankind, the society, the community). The directionality of relationship between church attendance and political efficacy may initially seem a bit puzzling given our earlier finding that church attendance predicted to *lower* rates of political participation (see Table 3). This issue is statistically resolved by the *negative* zero-order correlation ($r = -.28$) between frequency or electoral/non-electoral participation and political efficacy, a finding which conflicts not only with much previous research but with the criterion relationship often (mistakenly) employed for asserting the construct validity of political efficacy.[34] From a theoretical perspective, it may be that the "otherworldliness" of the ghetto church leads to an idealized (high) and comfortable sense of political efficacy which retreats from any reality-testing (that is, active participation). Regarding the relationship between the type of referent articulated for entering politics and political efficacy, it appears quite simply that in our Black sample those who enter politics for narrow, personalized reasons (such as getting a job, avoiding a draft call, having bail lowered for an incarcerated relative or friend) achieve higher feelings of effectiveness than those who enter politics on behalf of large numbers of people (to change the world, achieve racial harmony, restore ecological balance). Not only are behaviors which reflect narrow referents more concrete (therefore, more susceptible to quick feedback) but they are perhaps less likelty to be guided by the kinds of unrealistic expectations which the political system routinely deflates. That this relationship stands only for our Black sample, however, signifies that the explanation is still more complex, requiring the observer to consider, in some way, the systemic level as well.

For Appalachians, subjective feelings about "success" in past political experiences is the single best predictor of political efficacy, a relationship so clear in meaning that no further elaboration is required. Inexplicably, however, this variable was *not* a significant predictor of political efficacy in our Black sample (small zero-order correlation, r = .16). Income, also, is a predictor of political efficacy among our Appalachian sample; cash "in hand" may provide an individual with a tangible sense of power. If the folklore about the buying of political favors and votes is even partially true for the southern Appalachian region, we should not be surprised to find the wealthier having a higher sense of political efficacy, though the political utility of money can undoubtedly be expressed in more subtle ways. Finally, being in a farming-related (rather than non-farming) occupation contributes to *low* political efficacy, a finding which could reflect, among other things, the equally inept agricultural policies of both Republican and Democratic national administrations, the seemingly uncontrollable forces which affect the success or failure of farming (the weather), or the human isolation which characterizes farming in the United States today.[35]

For Indians, the division of the sample into subgroups provides quite interesting, if highly tentative, results. For those Indians who have participated in political activities beyond voting, success in past experiences is the single best predictor of high political efficacy (as in the Appalachian sample). The association between employment status and political efficacy, however, is a peculiar one. While one might expect that being unemployed (an indicator of unstable occupational history) would, if anything, lead to low political efficacy, our data indicate exactly the opposite relationship for participant Indians.

For those Indians who have not participated in political activities beyond voting, high Redness and frequent voting in non-tribal elections are both significant predictors of high political efficacy. The link between Redness and efficacy is not fully clear, though it may be that relatively "white" Indians feel alienated in the social structure of the reservation which emphasizes "Indianness" and that this alienation spills over into the political realm. In view of our general theory concerning the hypothesized distinctiveness of "politics" from voting, the finding that voting frequency contributes to *political* efficacy is an unexpected one. Yet, as we will discuss in a later section on voting efficacy, politics and voting seem least distinct for the Indian sample, both behaviorally and attitudinally.

The most dramatic finding from our Indian sample concerns the difference in the *class* of predictors which emerged for participants and non-participants. For Indians who enter the wider political arena, the influence of their cultural and social background is mostly washed out. It is not important (for understanding differences in political efficacy) how Red or rich or well-educated an Indian is, but at least partially—how successful his political experiences are (subjectively) and at what level of politics he takes part (national or local). In this light, participation can be seen to have a very "democratic" effect; individual differences (in personal background) are, to a large extent, neutralized. In stark contrast, culture (Redness) remains a powerful predictor for those Indians who do not enter the wider political arena. Indeed, this is strange support for the idea that one will lose his "Indianness" by participating in politics (white man's activity). More to the point, it is powerful support for our alternative model of political socialization—the attitudinal impact of participation is in no way more clearly demonstrated than in the contrasting forces which shape the generation of political efficacy among our two subgroups of Eastern Cherokee Indians.

In one final way, we can attempt to document the unique effectiveness of the frequency and context of participation in explaining variations in levels of political efficacy. In order to counter the argument that the portion of variance which participation variables explain overlaps that of background variables alone, a separate stepwise multiple regression was performed for each group on political efficacy, but including as potential predictors *only background variables*. Thus, we can measure the increase in the proportion of variance explained (R^2) attributable to the inclusion of the participation variables, and whether this increase is statistically significant.[36] Table 5 presents the comparative results.

The results from Table 5 are ambiguous. In each of the samples, the increase in variance explained—when participation variables are added—is 10 percent or more. However, because of the small sample sizes and the number of predictor variables added, the resultant increases do not reach typically accepted standards of statistical significance. It is clear that background variables alone are inadequate for explaining variations in political efficacy within the three samples; there is some evidence, though

TABLE 5
Stepwise Multiple Regression: Comparative Runs for
Assessing the Independent Contribution of
Participation Variables on Political Efficacy

MULTIPLE	BLACK		APPALACHIAN		INDIAN PARTICIPANTS[a]	
	R	R^2	R	R^2	R	R^2
BACKGROUND VARIABLES ONLY	.56*	31%	.46*	21%	.38	14%
BACKGROUND VARIABLES + PARTICIPATION VARIABLES	.65**	42%	.61**	37%	.51	26%
INCREASE IN R^2	...	11%	...	16%	...	12%
F - test	p > .20		p = .15		p > .20	
N	(50)		(58)		(34)	

a. The comparison of multiple regression runs is not possible for Indian "non-participants," since only one participation variable (voting frequency) could be included in addition to the background variables.
 * Regression equation statistically significant at .05.
** Regression equation statistically significant at .01.

far from conclusive, that the political experiences of individuals affect their sense of political efficacy.

VOTING EFFICACY

A second "attitude" which we tried to locate in the mental set of our three samples was voting efficacy—the degree to which individuals give primary or exclusive efficacy to voting as a political weapon. However, our factor-analytic procedures failed to yield a conceptually equivalent attitudinal construct for all three groups. For the Black and Appalachian samples, a reasonably clear voting efficacy factor (and unidimensional scale) emerged; for the Indian sample, our original Likert-type operationalizations of voting efficacy proved unrelated to one another; no factor (scale) emerged which could, by our standards,[37] be called equivalent to those which appeared for the other two samples. In sum, from a theoretical stance no distinct attitude representing voting efficacy could be isolated for the Indian sample; rather, operationalizations of political efficacy and voting efficacy interrelated in complex ways which suggest that the two attitudinal constructs for Blacks and Appalachians are but *one* for the Indian sample. This lack of distinction between politics and voting at the attitudinal level seems a reflection or reinforcement of a similar lack of distinction at the behavioral level—very few political activities outside the electoral arena were reported by the Indian sample as a whole (see Table 1).

Having made what must be only abbreviated comments on the issue of cross-cultural equivalence in the search for voting efficacy, let us turn to the results of separate stepwise multiple regression analyses on our factor-analytic "voting efficacy" scale for the Black and Appalachian samples. Table 6 reports the beta weights as well as zero-order correlation coefficients for the statistically significant predictors of voting efficacy for the two groups, and the multiple correlation coefficients (R) for the significant predictors taken together.

TABLE 6
Stepwise Multiple Regression:
Predictors of High Voting Efficacy

Predictors	BLACK		APPALACHIAN	
	beta	(r)	beta	(r)
PARTICIPATION VARIABLES				
NUMBER OF POLITICAL EXPERIENCES	-.64	(-.61)	---	
FEELINGS OF SUCCESS	-.21	(.12)	---	
% LOCAL EXPERIENCES	-.40	(.00)	---	
% COMMUNAL REFERENTS	.25	(-.05)	---	
% SYMBOLIC OUTCOMES	---		-.19	(-.28)
VOTING FREQUENCY	.25	(.30)	.25	(.02)
MEMBER - FARM BUREAU	x[b]		-.15	(-.16)
BACKGROUND VARIABLES				
AGE	.23	(.50)	---	
EDUCATION	---		-.43	(-.48)
CHURCH ATTENDANCE	.28	(.42)	---	
MILITARY SERVICE	x[b]		-.36	(-.37)
MARITAL STATUS	---		.22	(.24)
MULTIPLE R	.81**		.69**	
N[a]	(50)		(58)	

a. Pairwise deletion was utilized for missing data.
b. Data on this variable not collected for a given sample.
** Regression equation statistically significant at .01.

An overview of the data from Table 6 yields several important findings. First, quite different sets of predictors of voting efficacy emerge for the two groups: for Blacks, five of the seven predictors are participation variables including the two most important, while for Appalachians the two best predictors are background variables. Second, it is clear that the origins of *voting* efficacy are not the same as those for *political* efficacy in either group. While some variables do appear as predictors for both attitude constructs in a given sample, their directionality of influence is often reversed (such as percent of local political experiences, percent of communal referents). Thus, we have a second kind of evidence (beyond factor analysis) suggesting the distinctiveness of political efficacy from voting efficacy in the Black and Appalachian samples. Finally, the multiple correlation coefficients for the respective sets of predictors are very high. Fully 65 percent of the variation in voting efficacy among Blacks and nearly 50 percent of the variation among Appalachians is accounted for by the several predictors. In view of our self-imposed restriction to "logically prior" variables (such as personal background and past participation) in utilizing stepwise multiple regression on present attitudes, this is impressive evidence for the explanatory power of our model of socialization. Because of the large number of predictor variables which appeared in each group, we will highlight only the major findings and their theoretical import.

For Blacks, the finding that relatively frequent participation in electoral and non-electoral political activities leads to *low* voting efficacy is a fascinating one which, in retrospect, seems readily explained. By participating in many activities beyond voting and often outside the electoral arena entirely, individuals simply come to see that voting is only one of many ways to influence the political system; for a variety of reasons it may be the most cumbersome, indirect, and at times least appropriate method of attempted influence. Alternatively, one might argue that the data suggest political experiences are "alienating" in the sense that individuals come to see first-hand the electoral system for what it really is—through their experiences, many of which do involve the trappings of campaigns. Yet such an explanation fails to account for the *negative* predictive relationship (beta) between feelings of success in past experiences and voting efficacy—the *more successful* are one's past political experiences, the *lower* is one's present sense of voting efficacy. Thus, it is not that experiences necessarily expose vulgarity in electoral politics; rather, they seem to introduce a sense of perspective into the individual's perceptions of how the government and the political system work. The more often and successfully one utilizes tools of political influence other than voting, the less "exclusive efficacy" one is willing to attribute to voting.

But why not among Appalachians? While there is a small negative zero-order correlation ($r = -.17$) between the total number of political experiences and voting efficacy for this sample, the predictive relationship does not hold in the regression equation. And there is no zero-order correlation at all between success in past experiences and voting efficacy. If the impact seems so understandable for Blacks, the lack of effect for Appalachians is initially somewhat puzzling. One partial explanation might be that Appalachians are exposed to a *narrower diversity* of political activities than Blacks. Fewer Appalachians report such activities as picketing, protesting, and demonstrating; in general Appalachian political experience was found to be primarily electoral-related. Thus, the perspective about voting that Blacks seem to acquire through political participation may be less readily forthcoming to Appalachian participants. For the latter, background characteristics are the primary predictors of level of voting efficacy. Yet the directionality of relationships here suggests a somewhat parallel interpretation. Much formal education and military service are both depressants of voting efficacy. Thus, Appalachians seem to acquire a sense of perspective—a balancing of voting vis-a-vis other political weapons—through the *social* experiences of attending some college and serving in the armed forces. These, then, become "broadening" experiences (that is, experiences which take the individual away from home and disrupt the "normal" lines of parental socialization), much as political activity for Blacks.[38]

Finally, as we did for political efficacy, we can assess the statistical impact of the inclusion of political participation variables regressed on voting efficacy by comparing those results with ones from a regression including only background variables. Table 7 presents the findings.

The results confirm earlier impressions. Participation variables provide enormous *unique* explanatory power for variations in voting efficacy among Blacks, but much less (if any) for Appalachians. Nevertheless, feelings of efficacy or inefficacy toward the institution of voting are not fixed early in childhood for either group. For Blacks, the frequency and context of adult political experiences are crucial; for Appalachians, it is the relatively late background variables (experiences) of additional formal education and military service which are most important.

TABLE 7
Stepwise Multiple Regression: Comparative Runs for
Assessing the Independent Contribution of
Participation Variables on Voting Efficacy

	BLACK		APPALACHIAN	
MULTIPLE	R	R^2	R	R^2
BACKGROUND VARIABLES ONLY	.62*	38%	.63***	40%
BACKGROUND VARIABLES + PARTICIPATION VARIABLES	.81**	66%	.69**	48%
INCREASE IN R^2	...	28%	...	8%
F – test		p < .005		p > .20
N		(50)		(58)

* Regression equation statistically significant at .05.
** Regression equation statistically significant at .01.
*** Regression equation statistically significant at .001.

SUMMARY AND COMMENT

In reviewing these findings, it seems clear that the two hypotheses derived from the methodological arguments which guide this research have received considerable empirical support. None of the three groups resembles closely any national profile of Americans in their political activity. For example, if we refer to Milbrath (1965) for a baseline about political participation *levels*, the number of equivalent "gladiators" in our samples of Blacks, Appalachians, and Indians far exceeds his 5-7 percent range. Among Blacks and Appalachians, the activist ranks are perhaps as much as three times greater than that range,[39] differences which cannot entirely be accounted for either by the "sex-bias" of our samples (only male) or the expansion of the definition of political participation itself (to include non-electoral activities). Most significantly, in some important aspects of the political lives of Black, Appalachian, and Indian Americans, "systems differ." Not only do the distributions of selected political phenomena differ among the three groups, but the variable interrelationships surrounding these phenomena also differ. In some instances, widely different classes of predictors emerged to explain an "equivalent" phenomenon across the three groups. In other instances, the directionality of variable interrelationships was reversed from group to group, suggesting the need to examine systemic (group) level forces—the role of the church in the Black and Indian communities, the functions of income in all three groups, and the nature of the three local political systems from which our samples were generated.

Two methodological questions, raised by the theory and design of this research, might be speculated upon briefly. First, how different is "different?" How different do groups have to be from one another before subgroup analysis within the United States is, in some methodological sense, "required" or desirable? At what point do "political cultures" begin and end? What are the *criteria* by which judgments about the import of (cultural) group differences are to be made? In the broadest form, these questions allow no easy formulas. Simple statistical notions related to "chance" seem of little potential value. It may even be that refined quantitative notions will prove insufficient to this task. Raising the *question* may be a kind of theoretical advance which will, in turn, stimulate new kinds of research in the methodology of cross-cultural differences and similarities.

Nevertheless, a few things may be said about the extent of differences among our samples of Blacks, Appalachians, and Indians, or at least how "close" in political space each group seems to be to the other. Blacks and Appalachians, for example, are more alike than either group is to Indians with respect to the frequency of political participation, both electoral and non-electoral. The same space-distance pattern appears for the *structure* of political attitudes: among both Blacks and Appalachians, political efficacy and voting efficacy are empirically distinct political attitudes (as evidenced from factor analysis), whereas for Indians the two attitudes merge into one. In several variable pattern interrelationships, however, Appalachians seem to parallel their Indian neighbors, with the Black sample "different" from both. For example, the predictive (partial) relationship between income and the frequency of political participation is similar (positive) for Appalachians and Indians, but different (negative) for Blacks. Also, the impact of local political experiences on political efficacy operates in one direction for Blacks (positive), but in the other direction for Appalachians and Indians (negative). And then, the correlates of voting efficacy for the Black and Appalachian samples reveal some sharp contrasts (political forces versus social forces). Finally, the church attendance-participation relationship reveals no similarity among any of the pairs of groups and one pattern reversal (Black-Indian). In sum, the Black sample is sometimes similar to the Appalachian sample, and the Appalachian sample is sometimes similar to the Indian sample. But the Black-Indian dyad, in contrast, represents differences consistent over almost all areas of political participation and political attitudes. Why this should be so is not theoretically clear, especially because Blacks and Indians would be expected to have the stronger in-group identities,[40] and do in fact share a *common base* for their cultural identity (race, as opposed to geographic region). To get to these and other like questions, it may be that the "pairing" of cultural groups for analysis of similarities and differences (with at least conceptual analogs in mathematics or statistics, such as vector space analysis) is one path worth pursuing. But the search for an answer to that perplexing question about differences and "differences" surely lies far down the road.

A second methodological issue which is inevitably raised given the design of this research is the question of generalizability. In this study, we have but one sample of three groups of Americans, each sample drawn from different communities in different states. To what extent are the differences which we have found rooted, not in cultural variation, but in the varying locales chosen to "represent" these groups? How much is a function of the peculiarities of local political systems? How much is a function of urban-rural differences?

In one sense, these are worthy questions for which no immediate answers can be provided in the absence of replication by future researchers. Yet in another sense, the idea of "generalizability" can be distorted if pushed too far. Given the previously articulated methodological criticisms of the voting behavior and mass political participation research, in what way does it make *theoretical* sense to strive to "generalize" either to "Americans" or even to large heterogeneous cultural groups which may exist nationally only in statistical skeleton? The potential distortions of the legitimate role of generalization have been implicitly recognized in other social science disciplines and in some subfields of political science by those who have engaged in "community studies."[41] This may draw the line too sharply and divisively between those who study social phenomena in the United States through national sampling and those who study such phenomena *in situ,* in local communities, since both strategies have iconoclastic as well as complementary value in social research. But in the area of mass political behavior, it appears that the "national sampling" strategy has predominated to an overwhelming degree for reasons which are not entirely clear and with consequences which have not been thoroughly explored or debated.

Beyond the methodological arguments of this research, one major theoretical framework was developed to integrate the various strands of data collected through survey research: a model of political socialization focusing on the importance of adult participation in politics as a crucial intervening variable between one's personal heritage and present political attitudes. Various stepwise multiple regression analyses tend to indicate that such a model does have a substantial empirical base in all three groups. Both the frequency and the context of participation affect in blunt, subtle, and culturally selective ways individual attitudes about potential effectiveness in the political system.

The notion that political socialization or political learning takes place after the "crucial" years of childhood and early adolescence has not been common among political scientists. At best, some concessions in this direction are made for extraordinary events (period or zeitgeist effects), but rarely for the more routine political experiences through which individuals pass. In part, the lack of longitudinal data has made these kinds of assessments difficult,[42] and the present research can only add more cross-sectional data to the debate. Nevertheless, the idea that the political cues which participation in its various styles offers can be a potent source of political socialization is one which can be easily explored if the seductive power of old assumptions and limited empirical findings can be controlled.

Finally, to return to our opening thoughts on cultural diversity and the history of the American experience: to the extent that there is some empirical support for the "ideology" of cultural diversity, what is the impact on the polity? The spectre of "separatism"—as an outgrowth of the recognition of cultural diversity—appears on the American horizon now, as it has already appeared in a more fundamental way in nations as "different" as Canada, Nigeria, and Spain, to name but a few. The revolution to integrate, once hailed, has been slowed and is now even questioned by spokesmen for and members of minority groups. Whether the idea of cultural diversity and its extensions can accomplish in this nation what the idea of integration could not accomplish probably depends, in the last analysis, on the uses of psychological liberation. If individuals are freed or free themselves from the tyranny of one national culture, *for what* are they to be free ... *to do what?* Public faiths are, in a sense, easily enough destroyed. The question becomes whether private consciousness and self-identity will be confined to personal life-styles or whether, as many observers (TeSelle, 1973; Dixon and Foster, 1971) optimistically hope, a new and somehow "better" public consciousness can be created.

NOTES

1. Litt (1970) notes the widespread appeal of the melting pot image in American history. For historical references, see pp. 169-170. For works which emphasize the persistence of ethnicity, at least in narrowly-defined political areas (like voting), see Glazer and Moynihan (1970), and Dawidowicz and Goldstein (1963).

2. There is a substantial literature on developing nations which indicates that when cultural diversity is minimized within nations, national stability is maximized. For a recent empirical test, see Morrison and Stevenson (1972).

3. There are some supporting data to indicate that Americans lack tolerance of unpopular viewpoints and/or lifestyles. See, for example, Prothro and Grigg (1960) for the area of civil liberties.

4. For a beginning challenge to the application of standardized attitude scales to subgroups within the population, see Jacob (1971).

5. The words "frequencies" and "patterns" are borrowed, with meaning intact, from Przeworski and Teune (1970). "Patterns" refer to the comparability of variable interrelationships (that is, independent versus dependent variables).

6. For example, Backstrom and Hursh (1963), a standard political science text on survey research, argue for the value of "distance" in social research, especially between interviewer and respondent.

7. The final selection of communities inevitably reflected a concern for logistics and access, in addition to cultural "representativeness." Two of the three communities are geographically proximate; the third (Venice) although distant was one in which the author had sufficient prior contacts in the community to assure successful completion of interviewing.

8. For a fuller discussion of the Eastern Cherokee Indians, see Gulick (1960); also, Ryan (1972b).

9. A housing unit listing was constructed for the two census tracts in Venice which comprised the highest concentration of Blacks: CT 2732 is 50 percent Black; CT 2733 is 39 percent Black (preliminary Census Data, 1970). From this listing, every eighteenth unit was sampled. Because this initial sampling pool failed to produce the targeted number of interviews (non-Black households, no Black *males*, refusals, and so on), a second sample was drawn, selecting every forty-first housing unit. In each instance, interviewers were given instructions as to which Black male to interview, should there be more than one living in a given household (unit). It is interesting to note that both CT 2732 and CT 2733 are part of a special low-income employment profile for the Los Angeles area in the 1970 Census, suggesting the appropriateness of our label "ghetto."

10. Because county highway maps do not include any *incorporated towns* within the county (of which there are three in Claiborne), one town—New Tazewell—was arbitrarily selected as an additional "bloc" from which units were to be sampled, the number in proportion to the comparative population (in housing units) of the town vis-a-vis the already-selected blocs. In both Claiborne County as a whole (1970 Census) and the sample, the approximate balance between incorporated and unincorporated residents was 1:6. Again, instructions were provided to interviewers in the case of more than one male residing in a household.

11. No field housing maps exist for the Eastern Cherokee reservation, nor could one have been developed given the size and terrain of the land. The Baker and

Revised Rolls, however, contain the names, addresses, and ages (among other data) of all Eastern Cherokee tribal members. From these lists, every tenth male (twenty-one years or older) living in the five major townships of the reservation was sampled. The few tribal members who live in an isolated and generally inaccessible township (Snowbird) about fifty miles from the major part of the reservation were excluded from the sample.

12. In light of the very small sample sizes, the decision to study only males seemed necessary if one were to treat men and women as potentially different "systems"—consonant with the larger methodological premises of the research design. From observational experience in the Appalachian and Indian communities, the personal and political relationships between husbands and wives seemed somewhat different: in the Appalachian community, husband-dominant; in the Indian community, more egalitarian. Further research in the transmission of political cues between husbands and wives in different cultural groups might prove quite fruitful.

13. After consultation with local experts and residents, I judged that the "culture gap," which was too great in the Black and Indian communities to permit me to interview, was mitigated in the Appalachian community by a commonly-shared "whiteness" and by my "student" status. The refusal rate was not ascertained in the Black sample; it was 14.7 percent in the Appalachian sample, 6.4 percent in the Indian sample.

14. One notable exception is Matthews and Prothro (1966) who also asked their Southern Black and White samples about political participation over the course of a lifetime.

15. Note, for example, the sharp drop-off in participation at the "congressional" level from the Indian and Appalachian to the Black sample. Other data collected on respondents' information level confirm the logic of this particular finding: not one Black respondent could give the name of his congressman, whereas more than 75 percent of respondents in the Appalachian and Indian samples could identify their congressman. While overall levels of information were quite comparable across the three groups, it appears that the visibility and saliency of the congressional level as a political access point varies sharply; this may be one instance in which the urban-rural locale of the three samples is a key determinant.

16. There are, actually, quite a few studies of local politics (such as Crain, 1968, 1969; Alford and Scoble, 1968; Keech, 1965; Dahl, 1961), but most of these works form a different substantive tradition (pressure group and pluralist politics) than the "political participation" literature.

17. 84 percent of the Appalachian sample reported voting "all the time" in local elections (county-level); 79 percent of the Indian sample reported voting "all the time" in local elections (tribal); only 27 percent of the Black sample reported voting "all the time" in local elections (city-county).

18. Several comments regarding the dependent variable should be reiterated here. First, as noted in the text, in all three samples there was a substantial correlation between the frequency of electoral participation and the frequency of non-electoral participation (Black, $r = .58$; Appalachian, $r = .42$; Indian, $r = .61$), so high that the decision was made to merge the two variables into one measure of political participation. (The need for this merging becomes particularly acute in subsequent analyses when the characteristics of participation become independent variables). Secondly, the interval score on participation is as much a measure of the *diversity* of political participation as it is a measure of the frequency of participation; this is so

because any individual might have engaged in a given activity many times, but only whether he has engaged in the activity *at least once* was the measurement criterion. Thirdly, the act of voting was *not* included under electoral-related participation; rather, it was separated entirely on the grounds that the routineness of the act and the repetitiveness with which it is typically performed mute any "experiential" dimensions analogous to those posited for the activities which do fall under electoral and non-electoral participation.

19. The use of multiple regression analysis with typical social science survey data represents some departure from standard practices in the literature. Four problems are raised by its use in the present context:

(1) interdependence of predictor variables,
(2) level of measurement of the independent variables,
(3) distributions of the variables, and
(4) missing data.

On (1), we have taken great strides to eliminate instances of highly or even moderately correlated independent variables through multicollinearity testing utilizing principal components factor analysis. As a result of these procedures, numerous variables (indicators) were dropped or merged or scaled. Yet the issues raised in Blalock (1963) and particularly, Gordon (1968) cannot be swept away with a few disclaiming sentences. The problems in interpreting (with reliability) the relative import of a number of individual or class of predictors for a given dependent variable suggest much caution; in general, caution has been intended in the text. Regarding (2), some of our independent variables are ordinal or even dichotomous-nominal measures, but many are also interval-scaled. The inevitability of the former in social science research should not, in this author's judgment, preclude the use of more powerful statistical techniques in the absence of convincing evidence that the biases from such uses outweigh the advantages gained in analytic interpretation and simplification. This position is generally supported by Gurr (1972) on pragmatic grounds, and by Labovitz (1967) after empirical testing of alternative numerical assignment procedures on ordinal data. Condition (3) is rarely met in the literature (except occasionally through standard scores). Nevertheless, highly skewed distributions on variables do present serious problems, both in the calculation of product-moment correlation coefficients and all subsequent manipulations based on such correlation matrices. In the present research, variables with extremely skewed distributions were not included in any multiple regression runs (such as the exclusion of "employment status" among Appalachians). Regarding (4), pairwise correlation matrices were produced because of the non-concentrated character of the missing data. Mackelprang (1970) finds evidence that pairwise correlational procedures are quite effective in minimizing bias from missing data (compared with other widely used procedures, such as estimation, neutral or mean scores), though more so with larger than smaller samples.

20. While most of the churches in all three communities are Baptist, this in itself would not preclude differing "ideologies." Unlike Catholicism, for example, the Baptist denomination encourages decentralization enabling individual congregations wide latitude in developing their own interpretations of Christianity.

21. There is a moderate *positive* zero-order correlation between income and frequency of voting in various levels of elections in the Black sample (r ranges from .25 to .45). For an in-depth discussion of the potential antagonisms between middle-class and "under-class" Blacks, see Frazier (1957).

22. The variable "education" refers to the respondent's own level of education, whereas "income" was measured as *family* income; thus, working wives could confound the meaning of the relationship between the two variables, especially in the Black sample where the (numerous) single respondents were likely to have a higher educational level than the married respondents (a relationship itself confounded by age, and so on). Also, in each of the samples, the problem of attenuated variance contributes an unknown into the assessment of correlation coefficients.

23. We do not intend to press the partial relationship between education and political participation in the Black sample (and the lack of such a relationship in the other two samples) because the zero-order correlation between those two variables is moderately high in all three samples (Black, r = .42; Appalachian, r = .31; Indian, r = .35). Problems with multicollinearity (income versus education in the Appalachian and Indian samples) suggest this caution.

24. For a review of the possible meanings of the variable "age" in political research, see Klecka (1971).

25. In the Black sample, 56 percent of the total number of political experiences reported occurred within four years preceding the interview; in the Appalachian sample, 39 percent; in the Indian sample, 46 percent.

26. In our Eastern Cherokee sample, eight men (14 percent) reported that they had once sought elective political office (such as tribal council, school board, vice chief). The respective ages at which these eight men first ran for office are, in ascending order, (asterisk denotes elected): 26*, 37*, 41, 41*, 46, 47*, 59*, 66*. Of particular interest, the two men who were under forty when first seeking office had twelve and sixteen years of formal education respectively, whereas for those over forty at the time of their first seeking office, five men had ten years or less education, and the sixth, twelve years. In searching through the literature on political recruitment for a possible comparison with white society, we found relevant Barber (1965). Recalculating some of Barber's crosstabulations, it was found that 55 percent of all his first-term Connecticut state legislators were *under forty* at the time of their *successful* campaign (and in some cases, undoubtedly younger in an earlier unsuccessful campaign), indicating that low-level political offices may be primarily a young man's game in white society. By contrast (albeit with very small numbers), only two of the six successful candidates for office among the Eastern Cherokee were under forty at the time of first election, and *both* of these had very high levels of formal education (compared with other tribal members). Thus, there appears some intriguing if highly tentative support for our idea that youth defers to age in the seeking of political leadership roles on reservations, except in those instances where the youth are well educated.

27. Although data were collected on the number of children for Black respondents, the large percentage of "single" respondents—never married (35%)—limits the utility of this variable in any analytic manipulations.

28. In these and subsequent multiple regressions, we have taken care to watch closely the ratio between the number of independent variables included in a run and the number of cases for the run. Blalock (1960) and others have warned that as the number of independent variables "approaches" the number of cases, the multiple correlation coefficient (R) becomes artificially inflated. Some (Ezekiel and Fox, 1959) have suggested the use of a corrected R under these circumstances. While not presented in the text, we can report that such a correction formula affects only slightly most of our multiple correlation coefficients, the exceptions being the

regressions based on the two subsamples of Indians (participants versus non-participants) where it was already noted to beware because of small numbers.

29. For recent discussions of the SRC scale, see Balch (1971) and Jacob (1971). In different ways, both attack the purported unidimensionality of the SRC Political Efficacy scale.

30. The technical procedures of attitude scale construction utilized here (in the context of cross-cultural equivalence) follow closely those in Jacob (1971).

31. In both of these last two situations, the "level" and "why" aspects of the context of participation, it makes little sense to choose in advance among the competing hypotheses since previous research provides few if any clues as to *how* to choose.

32. For example, our data reveal that among those Black respondents who attended a political meeting or rally (n = 25), 27 percent did not know anyone personally at the event for which they gave particular recall; in contrast, among Appalachians and Indians who attended a political meeting or rally every participant knew at least one other person at the event, and most often he knew nearly everyone.

33. Eisinger (1973) finds empirical evidence to indicate that "responsiveness" of local communities is related (in a curvilinear way) to the frequency of organized protests in the community.

34. This illustrates the danger in using "external" variables to validate the content of an hypothesized attitude. In the present instance, systemic-level influences seem to affect the relationship between political efficacy and the frequency of political participation. Among Appalachians, the zero-order correlation between the two variables is .36; among Indians, −.08. Thus, the relationship between political efficacy and participation varies sharply by group. Theoretically, while inefficacy in politics is typically associated with apathy in the society generally, among Blacks (and Indians) it is not—suggesting the importance of considering cultural groups (systems) separately.

35. For an excellent discussion of agrarian political behavior, see Campbell et al. (1964).

36. There is an available F-test which statisticians use to measure whether the differences in proportion of variance explained between two multiple correlation coefficients (R) are statistically significant when the number of independent variables in each equation differs:

$$F = \frac{(R_1^2 - R_2^2)(N - m_1 - 1)}{(1 - R_1^2)(m_1 - m_2)}$$

where . . . R_1 = multiple R for the equation with larger number of predictor variables

R_2 = multiple R for the equation with smaller number of predictor variables

m_1 = larger number of predictor variables

m_2 = smaller number of predictor variables

37. Cronbach's Alpha was used to test the reliability (homogeneity) of the factor-analytic scales. A coefficient of .70+ was treated as the minimum acceptable evidence for unidimensionality—that is, the presence of the hypothesized attitude. For the political efficacy scales, alpha = .73 for the Black and Indian samples, .79 for the Appalachian sample. For the voting efficacy scales, alpha = .75 for the Black sample, .73 for the Appalachian sample. For the Indian sample, the original (hypothesized) voting efficacy items reflected an alpha of only .37, and no substantial improvement could be derived through factor analysis either on the reliability front or on the issue of conceptual equivalence (validity). For a discussion of the Alpha coefficient, see Cronbach (1951), Bohrnstedt (1969).

38. The idea of "military service" as a significant political variable for this study emerged too late for inclusion in the Black interview schedule; nonetheless, it was decided to collect and use such data for the remaining Appalachian and Indian samples. Consequently, our interpretations in this section must be qualified slightly, to the extent that military service might also prove a significant socializer of Black attitudes toward the institution of voting.

39. For one summary measure of the extent of overlapping political activism within each of the three samples, see the CPA Index in Table 1.

40. Our data do, in fact, support such an expectation. In response to the Likert-type statement, "Often, I feel more proud to be Black/Appalachian/Indian than American," 88 percent of the Black sample agreed, 61 percent of the Indian sample agreed, but only 19 percent of the Appalachian sample agreed.

41. For example, see Crain (1968, 1969); Gans (1962); Dahl (1961); Hunter (1953); Whyte (1943); Warner (1941).

42. Two notable exceptions to the lack of longitudinal data bases in political socialization research are Jennings and Niemi (1973) and Newcomb et al. (1967).

REFERENCES

ALFORD, R. and H. SCOBLE (1968) "Sources of local political involvement." Amer. Polit. Sci. Rev. 62 (December): 1192-1207.

ALKER, H. R. (1965) Mathematics and Politics. New York: Macmillan.

ALMOND, G. A. and S. VERBA (1963) The Civic Culture. Boston: Little, Brown.

BACKSTROM, C. H. and G. D. HURSH (1963) Survey Research. Evanston: Northwestern Univ. Press.

BALCH, G. T. (1971) "Multiple indicators in survey research: the concept 'sense of political efficacy.'" Paper delivered at the Amer. Polit. Sci. Assn. Annual Meetings. Chicago.

BARBER, J. D. (1965) The Lawmakers. New Haven: Yale Univ. Press.

BERELSON, B. R., P. F. LAZARSFELD, and W. N. McPHEE (1954) Voting. Chicago: Univ. of Chicago Press.

BLALOCK, H. M. (1963) "Correlated independent variables: the problem of multicollinearity." Social Forces 42 (December): 233-37.

——— (1960) Social Statistics. New York: McGraw-Hill.

BOHRNSTEDT, G. W. (1969) "A quick method for determining the reliability and validity of multiple-item scales." Amer. Soc. Rev. 34 (August): 542-48.

BRIM, O. G. and S. WHEELER (1966) Socialization after Childhood. New York: John Wiley.

CAMPBELL, A., P. E. CONVERSE, W. E. MILLER, and D. E. STOKES (1964) The American Voter. New York: John Wiley.

CLARK, K. B. (1965) Dark Ghetto. New York: Harper & Row.

CLEAVER, E. (1968) Soul On Ice. New York: Dell.

CRAIN, R. L. (1969) The Politics of Community Conflict: The Fluoridation Decision. New York: Bobbs-Merrill.

––– (1968) The Politics of School Desegregation. Chicago: Aldine.

CRONBACH, L. J. (1951) "Coefficient alpha and the internal structure of tests." Psychometrika 16 (September): 297-334.

DAHL, R. A. (1961) Who Governs? New Haven: Yale Univ. Press.

DAWIDOWICZ, L. S. and L. J. GOLDSTEIN (1963) Politics in a Pluralistic Democracy: Studies of Voting in the 1960 Election. New York: Inst. of Human Relations Press.

DELORIA, V. (1969) Custer Died for Your Sins. New York: Avon.

DIXON, V. J. and B. FOSTER [ed.] (1971) Beyond Black or White: An Alternate America. Boston: Little, Brown.

EASTON, D. and J. DENNIS (1969) Children in the Political System. New York: McGraw-Hill.

EDELMAN, M. J. (1964) The Symbolic Uses of Politics. Urbana: Univ. of Illinois Press.

EISINGER, P. K. (1973) "The conditions of protest behavior in American cities." American Polit. Sci. Review 67 (March): 11-28.

EZEKIEL, M. and K. FOX (1959) Methods of Correlation and Regression Analysis. New York: John Wiley.

FRAZIER, E. F. (1957) Black Bourgeoisie. Glencoe: Free Press.

GANS, H. J. (1962) The Urban Villagers. New York: Free Press.

GLAZER, N. and D. P. MOYNIHAN (1970) Beyond the Melting Pot. Cambridge: MIT Press.

GORDON, R. A. (1968) "Issues in multiple regression." Amer. J. of Soc. 73 (March): 592-616.

GRAHAM, H. D. and T. R. GURR [eds.] (1969) Violence in America: Historical and Comparative Perspectives. New York: Bantam.

GREENSTEIN, F. I. (1965) Children and Politics. New Haven: Yale Univ. Press.

GULICK, J. (1960) Cherokees at the Crossroads. Chapel Hill: Inst. for Research in Social Science.

GURR, T. R. (1972) Politimetrics. Englewood Cliffs: Prentice-Hall.

HESS, R. D. and J. V. TORNEY (1967) The Development of Political Attitudes in Children. Chicago: Aldine.

HOFFER, E. (1951) The True Believer. New York: Harper & Row.

HUNTER, F. (1953) Community Power Structure. Chapel Hill: The Univ. of North Carolina Press.

HYMAN, H. (1959) Political Socialization. New York: Free Press.

JACKSON, G. (1970) Soledad Brother: The Prison Letters of George Jackson. New York: Bantam.

JACOB, H. (1972) "Contact with government agencies: a preliminary analysis of the distribution of government services." Midwest J. of Polit. Sci. 16 (February): 123-46.

––– (1971) "Problems of scale equivalency in measuring attitudes in American subcultures." Soc. Sci. Q. 52 (June): 61-75.
––– (1969) Debtors in Court. Chicago: Rand McNally.
JAROS, D. (1972) "Biochemical desocialization: depressants and political behavior." Midwest J. of Polit. Sci. 16 (February): 1-28.
––– H. HIRSCH and F. FLERON (1968) "The malevolent leader: political socialization in an American subculture." Amer. Polit. Sci. Rev. 62 (June): 564-75.
JENNINGS, K. and R. NIEMI (1973) "Continuity and change in political orientations: a longitudinal study of two generations." Paper delivered at Amer. Polit. Sci. Assn. Annual Meetings. New Orleans.
KEECH, W. R. (1965) The Impact of Negro Voting. Chicago: Rand McNally.
KENISTON, K. (1968) Young Radicals. New York: Harcourt, Brace & World.
––– (1960) The Uncommitted. New York: Harcourt, Brace & World.
KLECKA, W. R. (1971) "Some strategies for seeking age relationships in political behavior." Paper delivered at Amer. Polit. Sci. Assn. Annual Meetings. Chicago.
––– and S. E. BENNETT (1970) "Social status and political participation: a multivariate analysis of predictive power." Midwest J. of Polit. Sci. 14 (August): 355-82.
KUTSCHE, P. (1961) "A Rorschach comparison of adult male personality in Big Cove, Cherokee, North Carolina and Henry's Branch, Kentucky." Ph.D. dissert. Philadelphia: Univ. of Pennsylvania.
LABOVITZ, S. (1967) "Some observations on measurements and statistics." Social Forces 56 (December): 151-60.
LANE, R. E. (1959) Political Life. New York: Free Press.
LAZARSFELD, P. F., B. R. BERELSON, and H. GAUDET (1944) The People's Choice. New York: Duell, Sloan & Pearce.
LIEBOW, E. (1967) Tally's Corner. Boston: Little, Brown.
LIPSKY, M. (1970) Protest in City Politics. Chicago: Rand McNally.
LITT, E. (1970) Ethnic Politics in America. Glenview: Scott, Foresman.
MACKELPRANG, A. J. (1970) "Missing data in factor analysis and multiple regression." Midwest J. of Polit. Sci. 14 (August): 493-505.
MATTHEWS, D. R. and J. W. PROTHRO (1966) Negroes and the New Southern Politics. New York: Harcourt, Brace & World.
MILBRATH, L. W. (1965) Political Participation. Chicago: Rand McNally.
MORRISON, D. G. and H. M. STEVENSON (1972) "Integration and instability: patterns of African political development." Amer. Polit. Sci. Rev. 66 (September): 902-27.
NATCHEZ, P. B. (1970) "Images of voting: the social psychologists." Public Policy 18 (Summer): 553-88.
NEWCOMB, T. M., K. KOENIG, R. FLACKS, and D. WARWICK (1967) Persistence and Change: Bennington College and its Students after Twenty-Five Years. New York: John Wiley.
NIE, N. H., D. H. BENT, and C. H. HULL (1970) Statistical Package for the Social Sciences. New York: McGraw-Hill.
NIXON, R. M. (1968) Presidential Nomination Acceptance Speech, Republican National Convention. Congr. Rec. 114, Part 20: 26881-26883.
POMPER, G. M. (1968) Elections in America. New York: Dodd, Mead.

PREWITT, K. and N. H. NIE (1970) "Revisiting the election studies of the survey research center." Paper delivered at the Amer. Polit. Sci. Assn. Annual Meetings. Los Angeles.

PROTHRO, J. W. and C. M. GRIGG (1960) "Fundamental principles of democracy: bases of agreement and disagreement." J. of Politics 22 (May): 276-94.

PRZEWORSKI, A. and H. TEUNE (1970) The Logic of Comparative Social Inquiry. New York: Wiley Interscience.

ROSENBERG, M. (1955) "Some determinants of political apathy." Public Opinion Q. 18 (Winter): 349-66.

ROSSI, P. (1959) "Four landmarks in voting research," pp. 5-54 in E. Burdick and A. Brodbeck (eds.) American Voting Behavior. Glencoe: Free Press.

RYAN, J. (1972a) "Myth and politics: political participation in three American subcultures." Ph.D. dissertation. Evanston: Northwestern Univ.

––– (1972b) "Styles of influence-seeking on a rural reservation: the Eastern Cherokee of North Carolina." Paper delivered at the Southern Polit. Sci. Assn. Meetings. Atlanta.

SEARING, D. D., J. J. SCHWARTZ, and A. E. LIND (1973) "The structuring principle: political socialization and belief systems." Amer. Polit. Sci. Rev. 67 (June): 415-32.

SHAFFER, W. R. (1972) Computer Simulations of Voting Behavior. London: Oxford Univ. Press.

STEINER, S. (1968) The New Indians. New York: Dell.

TeSELLE, S. [ed.] (1973) The Rediscovery of Ethnicity: Its Implications for Culture and Politics in America. New York: Harper & Row.

U.S. National Advisory Commission on Civil Disorders (1968) Report. New York: Bantam.

VERBA, S. and N. H. NIE (1972) Participation in America. New York: Harper & Row.

–––, and J. KIM (1971) The Modes of Democratic Participation: A Cross-National Comparison. Sage Professional Papers in Comparative Politics, vol. 1, Series no. 01-013. Beverly Hills and London: Sage Publications.

WARNER, W. L., J. O. LOW, P. S. LUNT, and L. SROLE (1941) The Social Life of a Modern Community. New Haven: Yale Univ. Press.

WELLER, J. (1965) Yesterday's People. Lexington: Univ. of Kentucky Press.

WHYTE, W. F. (1943) Streetcorner Society. Chicago: Univ. of Chicago Press.

JOHN PAUL RYAN is a Senior Research Associate with the American Judicature Society, an organization of lawyers, judges, teachers, government officials, and others interested in the effective administration of justice. Prior to that appointment, Dr. Ryan taught political science at Vassar College. He is the co-author of a computer-assisted instructional monograph, The Supreme Court in American Politics: Policy through Law. *Dr. Ryan received his Ph.D. from Northwestern University.*

APPENDIX A
Demographic Characteristics of the Three Samples

	BLACK	APPALACHIAN	INDIAN
	Venice, California	Claiborne County, Tennessee	Eastern Cherokee North Carolina
MEDIAN AGE (yrs)	33.8	43.2	48.0
MEDIAN EDUCATION (yrs)	12.0	11.7	9.5
MEDIAN FAMILY INCOME	$5000-5999	$6000-6999	$3000-4999
% Working Wives	42.1%	42.0%	30.8%
OCCUPATION:			
% Unemployed (excl. student, retired, disabled)	42.1%	3.9%	32.7%
Dominant Occupation	Operative	Farming	Operative
Types (Census Classfc.)	Craftsman/Foreman	Managerial/Prop.	Managerial/Prop.
MARITAL STATUS:			
Single	34.7%	14.0%	10.3%
Married	40.8	80.7	67.2
Estranged	20.4	1.8	15.6
Widowed	4.1	3.5	6.9
Median No. of Children (excl. "single")	2.1	2.2	2.9
MILITARY SERVICE (% Served)	NA	34.5%	63.6%
CHURCH ATTENDANCE (% "Regular")	17.4%	60.3%	32.1%
MEDIAN YEARS LIVING IN SAME COMMUNITY	13.8	39.8	42.2
N	(50)	(58)	(58)

APPENDIX B
Operationalization of Personal Background Variables

NOMINAL-DICHOTOMOUS	BLACK	APPALACHIAN	INDIAN
PLACE OF BIRTH, SCHOOLING	Southeast, Southwest (+)[a] v. all other United States (−)[b]	all other United States (+) v. Claiborne County (−)	off Reservation (+) v. on Reservation (−)
MARITAL STATUS	married, estranged, widowed (+) v. single (−)	married, estranged, widowed (+) v. single (−)	married, estranged, wid. (+) v. single (−)
EMPLOYMENT STATUS	employed (+) v. unemployed (−)	X	employed (+) v. unemployed (−)
OCCUPATION TYPE	X	farming (+) v. non-farming (−)	X
CHURCH ATTENDANCE/ MILITARY SERVICE	yes (+) v. no (−)	yes (+) v. no (−)	yes (+) v. no (−)
LANGUAGE SPOKEN	X	X	only Cherokee, Cherokee & English (+) v. only English (−)
ORDINAL			
FAMILY INCOME	$15000 + 12000 - 14999 10000 - 11999	$9000 - 9999 8000 - 8999 7000 - 7999	$6000 - 6999 5000 - 5999 3000 - 4999 under $3000
R's/WIFE's BLOOD DEGREE	X	X	3/4 + 1/2 - 3/4 1/4 - 1/2 1/4 -
INTERVAL			
YEARS IN DWELLING, COMMUNITY	0 - n	0 - n	0 - n
FORMAL EDUCATION, NO. CHILDREN	0 - n	0 - n	0 - n
AGE	21 - n	21 - n	21 - n

a. All "+" designations represent the higher coding score.
b. All "−" designations represent the lower coding score.

APPENDIX C
The Context of Participation

VARIABLE	OPERATIONALIZATION[a]
SUCCESS INDEX	Interval variable -- range 0-9. Includes, equally weighted, three indicators: (1) perceptions of emotion (i.e., was the political experience an emotionally satisfying one or not . . .), (2) perceptions of efficacy (i.e., did the experience achieve any goals external to the individual . . .), (3) perceptions of feedback (i.e., did anything positive or negative happen in the individual's life as a result of the experience . . .).
REFERENTS (% COMMUNAL)	Interval variable -- range 0-100%. Represents the scope or breadth of persons on whose behalf an individual perceives his political experience to be motivationally based. Initially coded into three categories: (1) communal (the larger society), (2) group (interest, racial, reference), (3) particularized (family, friends, oneself). For analytic purposes, "group" and "particularized" categories were merged into "non-communal."
OUTCOMES (% SYMBOLIC)	Interval variable -- range 0-100%. Represents the character of the outcome (goal) which an individual subjectively seeks from a political experience. Coded into two categories--(1) symbolic (abstract), (2) tangible (concrete). For example, within non-communal referent space, a symbolic outcome could be . . . to achieve racial harmony; a tangible outcome, to get more factory jobs for Blacks or Indians. Again, it is the individual's perceptions of the experience which define the categories--not which behaviors are, in actuality, more likely or less likely to elicit symbolic or tangible outcomes.
LEVEL OF ACTIVITY (% LOCAL)	Interval variable -- range 0-100%. Represents the level of government at which an individual's political experience takes place. Initially coded into five/six categories: (1) Presidential, (2) U.S. Senatorial, (3) Congressional, (4) Statewide, (5) Local, (6) Tribal. For analytic purposes, all categories above "local" were merged into "non-local;" where applicable, "local" and "tribal" were combined.

a. Data on these variables were generated from open-ended questioning.

APPENDIX D

Principal Component Factor Analysis—Orthogonally Rotated Solution

	BLACK				APPALACHIAN			INDIAN	
	1	2	3	4	1	2	3	1	2
BIRTHPLACE	-.269	-.037	.807	.028	.106	-.448	-.253	X	X
LOCATION OF SCHOOLING	-.125	.031	.846	.055	.024	-.038	-.079	.571	.003
YEARS IN DWELLING	.086	-.028	.009	.887	.044	.023	.801	X	X
YEARS IN COMMUNITY	-.221	.399	.111	.658	.115	.117	.705	X	X
AGE	-.367	.321	.319	.546	.030	.152	.820	.077	.497
EDUCATION	-.412	-.037	-.332	-.356	.445	.033	-.020	.428	-.159
INCOME	-.141	.304	.055	.254	.631	.262	-.109	.476	-.110
LANGUAGE SPOKEN	X	X	X	X	X	X	X	-.112	-.126
R's BLOOD DEGREE	X	X	X	X	X	X	X	-.216	.001
EMPLOYMENT STATUS	.139	.052	.732	.092	-.133	-.236	.164	-.008	-.010
OCCUPATION TYPE	X	X	X	X	X	X	X	X	X
MARITAL STATUS	-.360	.351	.085	.287	.016	-.097	-.057	.052	.164
NO. OF CHILDREN	-.275	.033	.093	.146	.114	.008	.060	-.320	.320
CHURCH ATTENDANCE	X	X	X	X	-.196	.204	-.159	.181	.057
MILITARY SERVICE	X	X	X	X	-.185	X	-.164	-.061	-.061
WIFE's BLOOD DEGREE	X	X	X	X	X	X	X	-.136	-.018
# ELECTORAL EXPERIENCES	.862	-.079	-.072	.026	.734	.293	.040	.868	.168
# NON-ELECTORAL EXPS.	.850	.036	-.186	.072	.722	.031	.005	.796	.138
# TOTAL EXPERIENCES	.967	-.024	-.150	-.060	.844	.242	.035	.928	.170
# RECENT EXPERIENCES	.686	-.030	-.093	-.132	.480	.080	-.591	.748	.114
SUCCESS INDEX	-.190	-.050	-.063	.049	.184	.006	-.035	.133	.051
% COMMUNAL REFERENTS	-.303	-.002	-.256	.387	.032	.157	-.097	.325	.067
% SYMBOLIC OUTCOMES	-.063	-.272	-.296	.096	.145	-.157	.103	.133	-.048
% LOCAL EXPERIENCES	-.194	-.153	-.004	-.055	-.305	-.328	.130	-.076	-.199
VOTE - PRESIDENTIAL	-.183	.923	.040	-.020	.228	.756	.020	.202	.893
VOTE - CONGRESS	-.016	.891	-.011	.172	.177	.682	.077	.021	.890
VOTE - LOCAL (TRIBAL)	-.097	.865	.020	.194	.058	.727	.165	.128	.213
VOTE - 1968 PRESIDENTIAL	.043	.830	.078	-.114	.141	.820	.022	.176	.851
# VOLUNTARY GROUP AFFILS.	.441	-.030	.193	.193	.773	.089	.213	.748	.113
MEMBER - FARM BUREAU	X	X	X	X	.187	.072	.613	X	X
MEMBER - COMMUNITY CLUB	X	X	X	X	X	X	X	.651	.073
MEMBER - AMERICAN LEGION	X	X	X	X	X	X	X	.300	.018

APPENDIX E
List of Independent Variables Included in
Stepwise Multiple Regressions on "Political Efficacy"
and "Voting Efficacy"

BLACK	APPALACHIAN	INDIAN
Place of Birth/Schooling	Place of Birth/Schooling	Place of Schooling
Years Living in Community	---	---
Age	Age	Age
Education	Education	Education
Income	Income	Income
Employment Status	---	Employment Status
---	Occupation Type	---
Marital Status	Marital Status	Marital Status
Church Attendance	Church Attendance	Church Attendance
---	Number of Children	Number of Children
---	Military Service	Military Service
---	---	Redness
---	---	Wife's Blood Degree
- - - - - - -	- - - - - - -	- - - - - - -
Success Index	Success Index	Success Index[a]
% Communal Referents	% Communal Referents	% Communal Referents[a]
% Symbolic Outcomes	% Symbolic Outcomes	% Symbolic Outcomes[a]
% Local Activities	% Local Activities	% Local Activities[a]
Voting Frequency (all elections)	Voting Frequency (all elections)	Voting Frequency (non-tribal elections)
Number of Voluntary Group Affiliations	---	---
---	Member – Farm Bureau	---

a. Included only in "participant" subsample of Indians; all other variables included for both subsamples.

APPENDIX F
Factor-Analytic Attitude Scales

Political Efficacy

BLACK

[a]"It doesn't do much good to go to court for things, because the courts are unfair to people like me."

[a]"In the world of 1970, votes don't speak loud enough; nowadays, you have to shout to be heard."

"Most of the time, the political decisions made in this country take into account the opinions of people like me."

"Most of the politicians in Washington won't listen to me no matter what I do."

"It seems the only way people can get the Government to listen these days is to use violence."

"It's sometimes good to ask yourself why you vote and whether voting is worthwhile."

— — — — — —

APPALACHIAN

[a]"It doesn't do much good to go to court for things, because the courts are unfair to people like me."

[a]"In the world of 1970, votes don't speak loud enough; nowadays, you have to shout to be heard."

"Most of the politicians in Washington won't listen to me no matter what I do."

"It seems the only way people can get the Government to listen these days is to use violence."

"Politics and government are so complicated that there is no way to catch the attention of the right public officials."

"It isn't important to vote when the candidates are pretty much the same."